Leading the Sustainable Sch

CW00552985

Also available from Continuum

Creating Tomorrow's Schools Today, Richard Gerver
Developing a Self-Evaluating School, Paul K. Ainsworth
The Primary Curriculum Design Handbook, Brian Male
Tales from the Head's Room, Mike Kent

Leading the Sustainable School

Distributing Leadership to Inspire School Improvement

DEBRA MASSEY

continuum

Continuum International Publishing Group
The Tower Building   80 Maiden Lane
11 York Road   Suite 704
London   New York
SE1 7NX   NY 10038

www.continuumbooks.com

British Library Cataloguing-in-Publication Data
A catalogue record for this book is available from the British Library.

ISBN: 978-1-4411-0915-6 (paperback)

Library of Congress Cataloging-in-Publication Data
Massey, Debra.
    Leading the sustainable School : distributing leadership to inspire School improvement / Debra Massey.
    p. cm.
    Includes bibliographical references and index.
    ISBN 978-1-4411-0915-6 (pbk: alk. paper)–ISBN 978-1-4411-2852-2 (ebook pdf : alk. paper)–ISBN 978-1-4411-8098-8 (ebook epub: alk. paper) 1. School management and organization–Great Britain. 2. Educational leadership–Great Britain. 3. School improvement programs–Great Britain. I. Title.

    LB2900.5.M37 2011
    371.200941–dc23
                  2011022995

Typeset by Fakenham Prepress Solutions, Fakenham, Norfolk NR21 8NN
Printed and bound in India

For Graham, Tom and Joe for being my constant touchstone with reality

Contents

Preface

From Tiny Acorns ... Great Oaks Grow

I start my new headship in September 2005 with no Deputy, a crumbling building and an undersubscribed School. The previous Ofsted had deemed curriculum and governing body as unsatisfactory and exclusions are historically high compared to the number of children on roll. Parents and colleagues are sceptical about whether the new School would ever be built, due to endless delays. There is so much to do and one thing is certain: when this state of the art new building is ready, a satisfactory School on an outstanding site simply will not do.

I felt an instant protectiveness towards my new School and the community it served, even as over the next few weeks more colleagues asked me why on earth I would move from my successful village School headship to such an appointment. Like the mother of a child not quite perfect, a fierce determination to bring this School, phoenix-like from the ashes was almost all-consuming at times. That might sound like I viewed turning this School around as a one woman show, but in leading by example whilst developing sustainable growth, I soon found out that my strategies required variation and extended team strengths. Certainly, a new attribute also needed to be implanted within my personal makeup ... patience!

As Head of a relocated School and new Children's Centre, sustainability of leadership through my combined roles was a real concern. Hence the determination to grow an organization with clearly defined roles and a shared vision, and this has been the focus of my role over the last five years. Key aspects of leadership will be explored through this book, in manageable and realistic chapters, rooted in common sense and real life examples. The references to the School website aim to support this with relevant research and press interest in Howe Dell, to reinforce its credibility. More usefully for those considering leadership at a time of change, a website linked to the book includes relevant case studies, planning and training tools to support that transition.

After 20 years in primary education, including various management responsibilities as Head and Deputy, my professional base broadened when I took up the position as Hertfordshire's County Adviser for Personal Social and Health Education for primary, secondary and special schools. The insight this role gave me in demonstrating the advantages of working with other disciplines for the benefit of young people was invaluable. It was during my time as an adviser that I experienced working in multi-agency groups on diverse agendas including Anti-Bullying, Healthy Schools and Drugs Awareness. Ironically, Hertfordshire was undergoing a huge cultural revolution: a move from single agencies towards a united 'joined up' service with the child at the centre – hence 'Children, Schools and Families' was born.

The Victoria Climbie Inquiry in January 2003 and the Every Child Matters agenda Green Paper 2003 were stimuli for working in multi-agency teams. It was not an instant success; nevertheless, it recognized that to make a difference to vulnerable children, a shared aspiration was required, to forge a way forward into multi-agency working as an ideal. From this, I learned that in Collins' words:

> Great leaders get the right people on the bus, wrong people off the bus and the right people in the right seats and then they figure out where to drive it.
>
> J. G. Collins, *Good to Great: Why Some Companies Make the Leap – and Others Don't*, New York: Harper, 2001, p. 13

Despite leaving the Advisory Service due to frustrations surrounding overriding bureaucracy, which at times stifled creativity, I nevertheless recognized two things:

♦ Working within and leading teams was something important to my professional role.
♦ I passionately believed in an holistic view of the child and the family being necessary, if true inclusion was to be achieved, and I wanted to shape that provision through the services I was able to lead.

Therefore, when the advertisement in the *Times Educational Supplement* asked potential candidates if they wanted to be Head of a two-form entry Eco Primary School with Children's Centre, a first in Britain, I was hooked! The now award-winning curriculum began as a draft plan which has been adapted to meet sustainable principles through an integrated approach. Education for Sustainable Development (ESD) principles are just as deeply embedded into the ethos of Howe Dell as Christian ideals were key to the Church School culture of my previous headship. The curriculum is available via the School website and the development of it is further explained in Chapter 10. It was vital that this plan evolved from the old site, prior to the benefits of the new build, thus proving it could have resonance anywhere.

On arrival, I discovered a 'tired' School with a six-year outstanding building project which had only half of the £11 million-budget allocated. There was a proportion of temporary or new staff that had very little understanding of what the Children's Centre would do beyond Day Care, which governors had been keen to manage in-house. Expectations of pupils were low and needed challenging in a way that *empowered* staff to be part of the newly emerging vision.

The original building was romantic (being Tudor in beautiful grounds) but impractical: one toilet for 60 pupils under the age of 6 … *and upstairs*!

I have described the Old Rectory building as 'like an elderly but much loved movie star from the silver screen: even today in the right light, from the right angle, for the right role, this building is reminiscent of a bygone age of romance and glamour … But likewise, in the wrong role and on closer inspection, its flaws are all too clear, it smells funny … And it leaks!'

The replacement building was 'state of the art' in comparison and bravely designed to encompass renewable energy systems, which might be a blueprint for future buildings. These included:

◆ a heating system that absorbs heat from the sun – this is stored and released to heat the School in winter;
◆ solar panels that pre-heat water for use in the School kitchens;
◆ photovoltaic panels that provide electricity;
◆ high-performance windows that reduce heat loss;
◆ design features which minimize the need for artificial lighting.

Following the earlier analogy with movie stars, like some of our new starlets of today, these may be fascinating and exciting to observe, but need careful management, and can at times demand high maintenance!

The journey and lessons to be shared
The first challenge was to recruit good staff on permanent contracts and in a year, seven of nine teachers, including Head and Deputy, had been appointed. Tackling teaching that was largely satisfactory, but some unsatisfactory, was key. At this stage, our Children's Centre was virtual and indeed had not even gone through the bidding process to become a reality.

The second challenge was to counteract the falling roll with positive marketing and high-profile access with parents: they backed away when every class was led out by the class teachers, assuming the children must be in trouble! Numbers rose from 150 to 274 within three years and the relocation to the new site took place. Getting to know those pre-school children and their carers at the School gate was crucial in developing a whole site vision and cemented our credibility with the wider community.

By now, a large majority of teaching was good, some being satisfactory, but *some also outstanding*. Looking back at my journal entry from 17 September 2007, I can see the dramatic change in expectation and the need for a directive leadership style. There is a clear understanding that many challenges are not always shared among the team, in an attempt to demonstrate clear direction. The actual diagram is avaliable via the accompanying website.

---

17 September 2007 – Lunchtime

Creating a visual Journey to Leadership didn't begin at the beginning: it began halfway across the page depicting a swan (as I'd aimed to be seen by colleagues) looking straight ahead to a vision of Every Child Matters. However, beneath the surface were frantic paddling feet, unseen by colleagues, who would not know what efforts this summer has demanded for us to open on time at a new high-profile eco School and Children's Centre. Perhaps, too, no one would notice that ahead remain large rocks entitled 'Building Project' and 'Staffing', whilst 'New Initiatives' lurk in the depths, hidden from view but ominous in magnitude and importance!

The successful Ofsted last week for the School and preparation for Day Care Ofsted tomorrow is depicted as a rainbow ... the first time probably in my career that I've actually felt I am capable in leading Howe Dell to be a School and Children's Centre of the future.

By referring to ongoing School self-evaluation as well as the community profile and needs analysis reports, it was clear to me that Howe Dell, on its new site, had a diverse community to serve. Both School and Centre contexts obviously share common ground, but they also have different priorities which needed to be understood and respected if the two organizations were to develop into one management model. Relevant data to support this baseline is available on the website.

Where is Howe Dell?

Hatfield has undergone a period of change that has been detrimental to the community. The loss of British Aerospace had an adverse impact on employment and left the town with many struggling families. As people found jobs elsewhere, houses were bought for the purpose of letting to university students. This reduced the number of families and thus the number of children in the town. As a result there are a significant number of surplus school places in the town and parents sometimes use this to avoid exclusion, by moving children with challenging needs from school to school.

Overall, Hatfield has five super output areas, which are among the worst 25 per cent in the region. Nine of the fourteen schools that make up the Hatfield Consortium are sited within, or have pupils who live in these areas, including Howe Dell. This area ranks third worst in Hertfordshire and is among the worst 20 per cent in England.

The rejuvenation of the town is being planned through the development of a large business park and a housing development of 1,600 homes on the old British Aerospace site. In addition, the University of Hertfordshire has built a new campus on the site.

More than just a school: transferrable leadership models have grown a learning community

A great deal of planning has gone into the Howe Dell project in the intervening years, as it is a high-profile development including a full range of services for under-5s, comprising a 60-place nursery and Day Care provision for children aged three months to three years.

Within a term, After School Club, Breakfast Club, Day Care and Children Centre groups such as 'Positive Beginnings' and 'Rhyme Time' all exceeded expectations in the number of children attending. There is a community hall on the same site which was much underused, and the whole design and build was to incorporate many sustainable and environmental principles and features.

Vast changes to the School's routines and expectations since September 2005 have impacted upon all aspects of the ethos of the School, which has had a direct effect upon the new School, Children's Centre and Extended Services. Numbers engaging in 0 to 5 provision and number of pupils on roll have increased, but so too has attendance in the School, which currently stands at 95 per cent overall. As you will read in later chapters, the motivation for this attitudinal shift came about through a creative approach and at times having the confidence to stand firm.

Many School staff have dual contracts and also work in the Children's Centre via our Extended Schools' or 0–3s' provision, a factor which was actively planned for and has already proved vital to enable a clear shared vision to evolve. Colour schemes, logos, even trees and resources, have all been decided upon with a holistic view and in consultation with parents, pupils and expertise beyond the School.

Strategies grow initially like weeds in a garden, they are not cultivated like tomatoes in a hothouse ... These strategies can take root in all kinds of places, virtually anywhere people have capacity to learn and the resources to support that capacity. Such strategies become organisational when they become connective, that is, when the patterns proliferate ... pervade the behaviour of the organisation at large.

Mintzberg, 1994, quoted by Beare, 2001, pp. 281–9

Minzberg's analogy seems highly relevant to my acceptance that growth will at times be haphazard, but there are great opportunities to consolidate current practice and cement the shared vision by using the skills and attributes of the people in my team.

A case study (outlined on the website) of a parent who juggled poor literacy skills with being a lone parent and ill health best demonstrates how her trust network developed, new skills were acquired and she later worked in the Centre and the School. This shows how creative leadership means looking at a dilemma and rather than seeing problems, instead seeks opportunities to support stakeholders, to have responsibility and pride in overcoming challenges. In so doing, ownership of outcomes encourages raised self esteem.

Many of the skills of leadership have been transferable from School to Centre. But how can this be developed to ensure ownership is not just at departmental level, but enables cross-phase opportunities for learning to happen? Hence my focus in growing leaders has been to facilitate the competencies of a talented team, not bound by traditional job titles and bureaucracy. The joy is that we are all learning together in a no blame culture, where leaders can be found at every level, thanks to personality strengths as well as traditional qualifications. There lies the starting point for distributive leadership, a view endorsed by Bergmann and Allenbrough:

> The diversity of School challenges leads us to believe that one person cannot solve all the problems in isolation. Individuals and groups need to step up to the plate to assume some leadership – once thought to be the realm of the Principal. (p. 97)

Section 1: Sowing the Seeds

1 | Growing Leadership from Within: Where do you Start in Developing a Team of Leaders to Raise School Success?

The School has a deficit budget, falling numbers on roll, poor SATs results and an ever delayed new School build: it is my first day at Howe Dell. As lunchtime looms the phone rings in my office and a midday supervisor asks 'Can the children go on the grass?'

Although I remember being somewhat bemused by this question, it has stayed with me for the last five years as being the perfect example of how leadership can fail. Why was it that a headteacher *inside* the building was expected to make a basic decision about playtime arrangements? The answer, quite simply, is because the inherited structure had been hierarchical – all decisions came 'from the top'. As a result, the School had lost its way, with senior leadership becoming way laid by day-to-day management decisions which, frankly, others on the ground were better placed to make.

On that sunny September lunchtime, it became apparent that my predecessor had worked very hard, but unreasonable expectations had been established that she should be the font of all knowledge; an exhausting role and certainly not a sustainable one.

Back to the story ... developing the midday supervisory role
Nevertheless, I walked out to meet my midday supervisor and a fidgety group of children, wriggling with anticipation of being 'allowed on the grass'. I ceremoniously placed my hand on the lawn,

nodded earnestly and declared play on the grassy expanse well and truly open. Amidst cheers and the clamour of children bursting onto the previously forbidden play area, I took the midday supervisor who had contacted me to one side and asked her how long she had worked at Howe Dell. She was frank about the behaviour of the children and her role as a 'small cog' and having chatted further, I watched how she managed her team whilst deflecting first aid incidents. I also heard how she also did the administration for the team: timesheets including overtime. This capable person was a team leader and as such, was given that role.

Key questions to ask at the outset

◆ How could we better use the skill sets of our staff in the School to not only empower them as individuals but to drive School development?

◆ Do we have an opportunity to establish a skills audit of our teams, beyond their paid role? (For example, we currently have a new teaching assistant who is a trained chef and played 'The Last Post' at our Remembrance Service on a cornet this year!)

◆ How do we *measure* the impact of making use of the whole person, as opposed to their delineated paid role, on the School and on the individual, thus encouraging ownership and growing leaders from within our organization? Investors in People and Staff Wellbeing surveys led by outside agencies can drive change, sometimes in a different way to that expected, but nevertheless offering a valuable insight into what it really feels like to work in the School. (The Howe Dell Investors in People GOLD accreditation report is available on the School website, for which the address can be found at the beginning of the book and on the companion website.)

◆ By encouraging broader skill usage, how do we *embrace* changes in roles and responsibilities, *without alienating* those who are comfortable in the currently established norms?

◆ How can a job description be modified to raise profile and ownership but to have clarity of protocol and line management?

Give time to grow relationships and listen to the message behind the words spoken

As Debbie and I grew to know one another, often joking about the fact we shared the same first name, I used to regularly joke that I got the salary, whilst she got the wet playtimes. Debbie proved herself to be a confident leader, clear about her expectations of the children (who respected her hugely), but also frustrated at the limitations of her team members' skills and understanding of their role within the building of a school of the future. Literacy skills and self-esteem was variable within the team; some behaviour from the adults was destructive, whilst others were passive, not wanting to 'rock the boat.'

At the end of the first week, I found 17 children sitting on the upstairs landing; I asked them why they were there. 'We've been naughty' they declared, some defiantly, some clearly not remembering which of their playground antics had been classed as 'naughty'. It transpired that whilst Debbie rallied her team using walkie-talkies, not everyone was playing to the team needs. The playground was off site, lovingly named the 'Bear Pit' by me, and accessed via a public footpath, but recognized as a potential 'pervert's alley', so policed by midday supervisors at all times. With these constraints, one key member of the team had taken to sending these 'naughty children' upstairs to avoid dealing with what were generally small misdemeanours.

What new learning emerged from this?

♦   Relationships take time to forge but it is time well spent.
♦   Change and development can occur through compromise and utilizing skills within the team that are not always immediately apparent.
♦   Team members need a sense of ownership in the process of change, if it is to be maintained and sustainable.

Consider how and when training can fit best with your team … and how messages and learning are delivered

Debbie and I talked about the growth and credibility of her team in whole site development, the sense of worth and understanding of the impact of their role. In response to this, I brought staff in early one morning, for paid overtime, to look at behaviour management. When behaviour is being mismanaged and impacting on learning, you cannot afford to wait – action needs to be swift, with clear directives. Some were militant and told Debbie they would not attend: after all, they had 'been doing this for years; who does this new Head think she is, telling us how to do our job?' All did attend, however, although body language varied from insecure to outright testosterone-fuelled aggressive.

The training began with a circle time ice breaker, to share what each enjoyed, if anything, about his or her role, followed by frustrations which hindered job satisfaction. Whilst the ring leader of the passive-aggressive brigade folded arms, rolled eyes and slouched, others tentatively began to open up: they wanted to make a difference, but felt they had no power. Some were clearly anxious in dealing with older children. One thing they all had in common was that they respected Debbie.

Giving the team a chance to draw diagrams showing the areas for which they were responsible, and to review what worked well while highlighting problem areas, also gave opportunities for others to take the lead, with a new recording style on offer.

The training was very active rather than relying on lots of writing or reading, as Debbie had protectively informed me that not everyone was confident in terms of literacy. This is something that can so easily be a barrier, especially to those in part-time positions in the School, notably those working in facilities or in midday supervisory roles. This does not mean that the person is unable to do a good job, and we must also guard against role stereotypes. In one school I worked at, I discovered one midday supervisor had a PhD, but was doing this job to fit around the needs of a large family!

What is important to note, is that consideration of different learning styles is just as important whilst working with adults as it is when working with children. I have a notoriously short concentration span in formal audio-led presentations; to the point that staff have joked it's like spending the day with a naughty 7-year-old. Perhaps this explains why I am sensitive to including different learning styles within any training for staff. After all, don't we do this for children, *so why should our work with our adults be any less inclusive*?

This philosophy has developed further as we have brought together large groups of staff members for training ranging from First Aid to Drama as a Vehicle for Learning, including midday supervisors alongside teaching assistants and teachers. This took a huge leap of faith by some, but in the longer term helped develop some midday supervisors into teaching assistants. It also stopped the 'us and them culture', which was very strong at Howe Dell in the early days.

Visual learners from School, Day Care and Children Centre teams chose to explore the outdoors through collage and photography, led by a teacher. This training was to reinforce outdoor learning in class and at play, through creativity, auditory learners learned to play steel drums, other options included dance and clay workshops.

Visual learners from School, Day Care and Children Centre teams chose to explore the outdoors through collage and photography, led by a teacher. This training was to reinforce outdoor learning in class and at play, through creativity.

How do you encourage growth and ownership, with scaffolding to support development along the way?

One powerful and negative member of staff, who is no longer with us, had the previous power invested in him removed, and he was directed to work with others (mostly Debbie or me) whilst other team members used role play to explore solutions to conflict. Disempowering the more direct and aggressive members of staff enabled our meeker colleagues to find a greater voice in shaping the future.

The session ended in a drafted action plan with agreed issues and possible solutions. Timescales and accountability were clear and there was an embryonic spark of excitement as we talked about further training, improved communication and clearer professional expectations. Keeping timescales tight and initially short-term engendered a sense of achievement and progress to be celebrated, however small.

The majority recognized they would be supported, but also that we were all there for the children and those who wanted to develop would have the support required to make that happen. There were tentative requests for further meetings, which we initially honoured each half-term. Later, these became one a term as there was less need for 'housekeeping'-styled meetings and more initiative from team members to resolve day-to-day issues. Remaining flexible when setting meetings, to ensure time for new ideas to bed in, while also regularly monitoring the impact of change, requires negotiation and – at times – patience!

Sometimes as a leader it is important to be an active listener and to also know when to hand over the leadership to the team leader: there remain things that will not be said to the Head, but which can be fed back by a capable person who represents a group at follow-up meetings. If this is to be successful, impact from the feedback needs to be tangible, otherwise the team will feel they are having little effect on change.

More and more midday supervisors began attending the training being offered for different groups of staff, as varied as Behaviour Management to Drama as a Vehicle for Learning. In each instance, staff received a certificate of attendance which was added to their professional portfolio. Furthermore, we began to encourage individuals to evaluate their training, whether it be in house or through an outside agency, and as a result they had to log what they would do differently in response to this new knowledge. This really raised both the profile of the individual and also the value of all training. It was yet another step in building the learning community we were seeking.

The variation of training will grow as the skills and confidence of the team members begins to flourish. Offering portfolios and certificates reinforces the importance of newly learned skills and reinforces professional development and credibility.

As the team developed, many grew into their new roles in a very positive way, whilst some moved on to pastures new, with the sometimes difficult task of facing competency and/or disciplinary proceedings. On other occasions, these newly empowered people used their skills in the wider community. By adding regular advertisements to our School newsletter as well as via recruitment websites, growing a team became less challenging.

There became a clear understanding that those successful candidates who were parents were appointed with awareness that they were not there to look out for their own child. In fact, we posted them deliberately to other areas within the School to begin with, not just to establish that parent and staff roles were not blurred, but also so that younger children especially were not confused. This was reinforced in our Staff Handbook, to ensure the new staff could focus on induction processes, as evident in our 'Professional Etiquette' section: 'Children belonging to members of staff should be treated like any other pupil. Therefore:

◆ The parent should not hear any details about that pupil's school day unless any other parent would be entitled.
◆ The parents are responsible for childcare arrangements beyond the confines of the school day. This might mean formally booking a child into on site after school provision or booking the child/children into off site childcare to fulfil duties outlined in his/her job description
◆ Teachers need to book Parent/Teacher Consultation appointments as any other parent would. No additional times should be given, nor should extended feedback be given in the Staff Room.
◆ First day cover for child sickness is covered at the discretion of the Head determined by the budget constraints and number of occasions, as well as health record of the member of staff'

The full 'Professional Etiquette' section clearly demonstrates a warm but open relationship between Head and staff, where expectations are clear and reviewed annually. This was welcomed by staff in ensuring personal and professional boundaries did not blur.

How did these changes impact on provision?

As time went on, there proved to be less focus on day-to-day management and more emphasis upon training and development of provision. By the end of the second year I no longer had any involvement in these meetings, with any relevant information being referred back in the leadership team meetings via Debbie. Today there continues to be a greater range of staff involved in making change happen, as the sense of self-worth and value of the job increases. Debbie's promotion to the leadership team was clearly explained to staff and governors, and the children never queried why this was the case: it made sense and ensured playtimes remained important to everyone's agenda. Happy playtimes meant a happy introduction for children to classrooms.

Playground buddies

We set about training pupils to lead games and clubs, and gave them the title 'playground buddies'. These children were charged with reinforcing positive play principles and to take responsibility for newly-acquired resources through a midday supervisory assistant budget. As their role progressed, some pupils were also trained in conflict resolution and the outcome of this – as well as positive developments in resourcing – were shared through whole-school assemblies and on our website.

The benefits were multiple, allowing the midday supervisory assistant to oversee larger areas, to review the effectiveness of new strategies and to monitor the engagement of vulnerable children. The children benefitted by having a greater say in what was available to them at playtime and, unsurprisingly, behaviour improved.

Growing the midday supervisory team

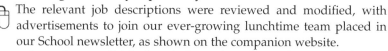 The relevant job descriptions were reviewed and modified, with advertisements to join our ever-growing lunchtime team placed in our School newsletter, as shown on the companion website.

As well as staff job descriptions, the roles and responsibility of Playground Buddies were publicized. These too are available on the companion website.

For many successful applicants, the benefits were twofold:

1   The work was less than 16 hours a week, so did not impact on benefits.
2   For some, it meant that they could venture back into the workplace after a gap due to having a family or long-term unemployment, but with hours to suit and term-time only.

Midday supervisory awards to celebrate exemplary pupil behaviour were introduced each term and published in our newsletter, meaning the status of dinnertime staff was raised even further. Did it all run like clockwork? Of course not, but having said farewell to two team members, new people arrived and this enriched provision. An example of these term awards for MSAs can be found in the following newsletter extract.

MSA AWARDS AUTUMN 2011

Congratulations to the following children who have been recognized by our lunchtime staff for their behaviour. We hope they enjoy their prizes.

Pupil Name	Reason for the award
Zarah, Year R	Always very well behaved
Georgina, Year 1	Very good manners in the Dining Room
Rachael, Year 4	Very helpful in the Dining Room
Sidney, Year 4	Always well behaved and polite
Peter, Year 6	Has been sensible in reporting incidents at playtime to MSA's
Saira, Year 6	Always helpful with younger children

Again, as this reward system developed and expectation of pupil behaviour was raised, polite behaviour became the norm for the majority and the awards began to include those who took responsibility for clubs, trying new or healthier food options, or the pastoral care of younger pupils. Prizes varied from Easter eggs to games or craft kits chosen from a *Crackerjack*-styled selection, to extend play opportunities at home. By giving pupils responsibility for themselves and their peers, and by raising expectation levels, children often respond by raising their own expectations.

Key points for consideration: Playground Buddies

◆ Empowering older children gives them a positive role, improves relations with midday supervisors, and choosing Year 5 means it could be part of class PSHCE provision. Hence there is efficiency here in time and resourcing 'killing two birds with one stone'. Training up Year 4 in the summer term, to ensure successful transition leadership, also ensures there is no slump in expertise and experience.

◆ Job descriptions for Playground Buddies makes it clear from the outset what is expected. Badges to mark this rite of passage need to be awarded prestigiously via School assembly, ideally with a governor or visitor presenting these. See the 'Roles and Responsibilities PowerPoint for Assembly and Job Description' on the companion website.

Creating an anti-bullying School?

Bullying – which at times was the worst I had ever encountered – became a rarity. At the end of our first year a playground buddy complained she did not have any playground issues to sort out anymore; people were not using the 'Buddy Stop', a place to visit if you needed a friend. Why? Because they did not need it! Playground Buddies were no longer needed to model good behaviour or find friends for children to play with because generally this was resolved by happy, occupied children. Hence playground buddies were replaced by sports leaders, whose focus was far more activities-based. These were trained and supervised by a designated member of the lunchtime staff and midday supervisors began to extend clubs and skills available at lunchtime.

Meanwhile Debbie continued to be invaluable, but not just for fire-fighting behaviour, as had been her focus previously, but now for managing a sustainable team. This reiterates the need for flexibility in responding to the current needs of staff and children. Furthermore, empowering the pupils in a positive culture of play and collaboration reduces the amount of time midday supervisors spend dealing with

Debbie enjoying whole staff INSET on creativity, alongside Midday Supervisory and Day Care colleagues (January 2010).

challenging or antisocial behaviour. This means they have more time to lead play and our midday supervisors report through performance management discussions increased enjoyment of their work. Did this mean bullying was eradicated? Of course not, but the team had swift support from teachers and leadership team members, who in turn got parents involved promptly. This raised confidence from the children that they felt safe at School and made it clear that behaviour from a small minority, which could detract from the wellbeing of the majority, simply would not be tolerated.

New site, new challenges
A year later when I was reviewing the transition to the new site, now ready for us to relocate, it was Debbie wearing a hard hat and builder's boots who came and visited the site with me. She and I created the risk assessments and agreed how the site would be accessed on the first day by buses as well as excited families. It was Debbie who talked through the pros and cons of how dinnertime would work (especially as only a third of the site would be safe and tradesmen were still working there). My role was to listen and to raise questions for her to suggest solutions to. This later included engaging our cook and other catering staff employed by the county council with strategies such as welcome lunches as part of our induction for new parents, and displaying vegetables and fruits used in the School dinner for parents and pupils to see ... The only hazard was sometimes a small inquisitive toddler might nibble at the selection!

Provision was reviewed regularly; when change took place it was communicated with clear reasoning via our weekly newsletter. Debbie stayed in her role supervising site access prior to the start of School and often resolved dinnertime queries with parents in a calm and friendly manner, alleviating small worries or concerns. Her success in managing adults resulted in her being encouraged to work as a group leader and outreach worker for our Children's Centre.

Resources

Resources do not always need to cost anything, nor do they always need to be sports-based. Consider how creativity can engage children at play, or refer to the recycling schemes to see if adventurous play can be introduced to a sterile playground, even on a shoestring budget.

◆ Try Scrap Store Play Pod for ideas, so long as you are willing to risk-assess appropriately first: www.childrensscrapstore.co.uk.

◆ Give old books a new lease of life as a 'story chest'.

◆ Ask for dressing up clothes and wet playtime games unused at home to be donated. Remember, engaged children will be too busy for disruptive behaviour, especially if they have ownership in what is provided.

◆ Set up a budget and enable midday supervisors and pupils to discuss needs and order items together for shared ownership. In most schools, midday supervisors work the least amount of hours for the least amount of money. Allocating even a small part of the school budget share raises credibility and engages ownership.

◆ Use a member of your midday supervisory team to engage with a selection of pupils in designing some playground markings – grids for hopscotch or targets for ball games, for example – initially in chalk to avoid an expensive commitment. Once the team of pupils and staff introducing these markings have established what works, then consider a sponsored event to raise funds to have these made permanent.

◆ In the same vein, investing a small amount of money in world maps or noticeboards for wildlife can provide a resource to use within the curriculum as well as at playtimes.

◆ Accept that items will need to be replaced, so encourage midday supervisors and children to audit the resources and build maintenance and replacement costs into their budget. In most schools, subject leaders have responsibility for a budget, so too should those responsible for playtime, either discretely through a play budget, or as part of the PSHCE allocation. In this way, spending can be with a named budget holder who is responsible for controlling this. However, since being a Head, even in lean years, I have always allocated a sum of money to 'school budget share projects', which is still curriculum based but loosely termed. It gives permission and financial capacity to 'think outside the box' or react to new, exciting ideas midyear.

◆ Playground Buddies should raise issues of broken or lost items in assembly – pupil power is a strong force and avoids midday supervisors being seen as the nagging adults. It is a powerful message that if we look after items, more will be possible. This is especially important in an organization which has sustainable principles. Sharing resources, reducing waste and considering cost over time, all encourage children and indeed staff to value the resources we have. It also promotes increased ownership, reducing breakages and extending the life of popular resources. However, it is worth getting a class at the end of a PE lesson, once in a while, to check hedges and such like for hidden items.

◆ With regard to **Performance Management:**

   ✓ Do performance management of midday supervisors as a group: they are only on site for six to seven hours a week in this role and it reinforces shared vision.

   ✓ As part of the induction process, basic training in First Aid, Child Protection, and Health and Safety should be made available for all, with a staff induction booklet including activities such as 'email your line manager in the first week' to share your thoughts and feelings of your first week in your new post. This task establishes where literacy or ICT help needs to be targeted. By doing this, barriers are removed and we can expect more from our teams.

   ✓ All midday supervisors should be encouraged to attend a whole staff INSET once a year. This should always be fun and has included drumming, Bollywood dance, art and drama as a starting point but reaffirms the whole-School vision of 'team'. It should be something that everyone looks forward to and planned to be suitable for a varied group with different learning styles.

Resources to facilitate training

We used training resources from various sources; from books such as *Making A Meal of It*, written by Jay Matthews and Roger Hurn by Pearson Publishing, and *Games For Playtime*, published by Devon County Council, to some homemade training resources based on what I had successfully used in other schools when I was an adviser. These are available on the companion website and include:

◆ Job advertisement extract from the School Newsletter. This advert encouraged some of our parents, often long-term unemployed, to return to the workplace through an organization they knew, in hours that worked within the school day and did not affect their family benefits as it was only part-time.

◆ 'Playground Buddies Roles and Responsibilities', written for use by Key Stage 2, to encourage pupils' voice in reviewing provision.

◆ Blank group performance management pro forma (see below for an example of a completed form).

For further information, PowerPoint presentations and projects please refer to the School website to review playtime development for staff and children.
Each midday supervisors' meeting resulted in a shared action plan, which at a later stage became a group performance management document, as shown.

Group performance management: midday supervisors' action plan, initially led by Head, later can be led by team leader

WHAT?	WHO?	HOW?	WHEN?
Training Target Huff and Puff Company training to lead play, utilizing Year 6 pupils	Year 6 and midday supervisor taking responsibility for this	Support from Sports partnership, using external links with other schools and equipment bought	Summer 2007 training, Sports leaders, Autumn 2007
Behaviour Target Behaviour management and activities: induction pack	Head	Pack given and copy in staff room	9 January 2008
In-house training	Head and midday supervisor team leader	'Buddy system' enabling new staff induction to encourage mentoring from experienced staff	Ongoing

WHAT?	WHO?	HOW?	WHEN?
Communication Target:			
To be developed because of needs of new site	All All DW and CD	DM to coordinate On order Follow the system	Ongoing September 2011 From January 2008
• Daily meeting			
• INSET days	DW → Class Teacher		
• Walkie-talkies	→ Middle Management team for F stage SW, KS1 CS or Deputy Head KS2		
• Behavioural issues			
Health and Safety Target Restraining a child/tackling difficult behaviour	All DM In-house training (needs driven)	Always with a professional. County training via Children's Centre for North Hatfield	Spring 2008

2 | Using Competencies to Build a Stronger Organization and Saying Goodbye to Stereotypes

'We can sit on this step all morning, but I wonder what fun we are missing in the classroom?'

'Who is that?' I asked my secretary as I looked out of my upstairs office window at a young boy, obviously angry and defiant, being quietly spoken to by a bowed blonde head. Everything in her demeanour was gentle and yet this boy, who was clearly ready for 'flight or fight', was listening to her. His shoulders were hunched, fists clenched and yet his foetal crouch was matched by the teaching assistant, who was quietly talking him down from wherever he had reached.

By mirroring his position while keeping her distance, she gave him space and dignity. Her patience in those 20 minutes on a cold concrete step resulted in him acquiescing to return to the lesson from which he had 'bolted'. He had dignity, he had been listened to, yet he had begun to deal with his anger and frustrations at life, as well as learning that these needed support and resolution.

I got to know this child very well in the next three years as he went into care, saw his world fall apart and yet with support from many at Howe Dell, a bright, high-achieving Year 6 pupil left us with the 'value added banner' waving high. Indeed he achieved at least Level 4s in all subjects, with Level 5s in Reading and Science – demonstrating over three years' good progress in the space of a few short months. Peter's full case study is available via the website, Case Study 2.

Yet for all Peter's achievements, what struck me on that morning were the skills of our teaching assistant. Some of these can be taught and modelled, but an intuitive response to a child in need was as natural an instinct to her as breathing, and this is a rare treasure indeed.

Professional development has its own time and journey. If an idea does not work first time, it does not make it a bad idea – possibly the timing is wrong.

Nina was a part-time teaching assistant who showed great promise and demonstrated many 'hidden' talents, beyond her prescribed job description. By searching for a chance to develop her skills, this actually resulted in losing her for a while … but she returned to Howe Dell with new confidence and aptitudes and is now a vital part of our leadership team. As budget allowed and her role developed, we have recently changed her from term-time only to a full-time contract. This would not have been feasible in a traditional school organization, but with a creative look at needs, rather than preordained job descriptions, a new role focusing on extended services and community partnerships emerged with huge professional responsibility – and continues to develop to meet the needs of Howe Dell.

Back to the story
Later in the week, I chatted to Nina about her work with this particular child and it became apparent that due to his behaviour he had missed playtimes and lunchtimes, which in turn made his pent up energy and anger a barrier to learning. I suggested that he might benefit from being given responsibilities at playtime (closely supervised) and also given planned 'time out to run and kick leaves' – to 'exorcise his demons'.

Often that autumn was punctuated with a view from my office of laughter and joint fun, as Nina and this pupil enjoyed the grounds with exuberance: this showed Nina's willingness to take risks and meet this child equally through the joy of play. Needless to say, he adored her.

Nina came to attention later in that first term as I happened to pop into a Key Stage 2 Songs of Praise Assembly to listen to a version of 'Twinkle, Twinkle Little Star', beautifully arranged, yet in a way unfamiliar to me. The musical arrangement was orchestrated by our new Music Subject leader and was sung confidently. Nina, however, was teaching the whole of Key Stage 2 how to combine the song with sign language. The outcome was magical, especially when later linked to solo voices in a performance to parents. When I asked about it later, she simply said it was nice to have the chance to use this skill. There was more to this teaching assistant than I had thought; whilst preparing for her performance management, I discovered she was also a graduate with a Psychology degree – something else which we could no doubt build upon.

Give yourself time to listen and learn from others: leadership does not always have to come from you!

One weakness of leadership can be that one's time becomes overfull without the chance to reflect or to listen to others.

◆ As well as taking time to talk to staff about their interests and life outside school, a formal skills audit (a template is available for you to use on the companion website) can be circulated on an annual basis at the same time as pecuniary interests data is collected each September. These can be collated and published in-house to ensure other people can utilize the artistic, sporting or other skills enjoyed by colleagues. It also avoids silos working without communicating between departments and in organization – that is, people only working with or being familiar with those within their immediate team.

◆ If new to leading performance management for members of staff, spend time looking at their file for their original application; it can also alert you to sickness or attendance issues and any other previous concerns.

◆ Celebrate staff successes, such as a sporting achievement outside school, as these good people could be excellent in supporting cross-country running in school and other new ventures!

◆ Remember, it is not always he or she who shouts loudest! Introduce staff training as a whole staff event or in smaller groups for larger organizations, with a circle time to share holiday news: it might be the first chance to hear that you have an ornithologist within your midst!

◆ Ensure that as well as pupil progress and professional development targets, time is allowed for leadership opportunities to be discussed. Leadership can be at *all levels* and may well prompt a teaching assistant to use skills from outside school to enhance extended provision. By doing this, we now have 'Let's Get Cooking', Craft, Art and Spanish clubs, all led by non-teaching staff.

◆ By asking if parents have a skill or interest to share, they too can contribute to provision, as clarified in later chapters.

How do you utilize the performance management to retain or extend good staff, break stereotypical expectations and enable School development to take place?

During performance management, Nina and I discussed the possibility of accelerated routes into teaching, as a means of enabling her to gain further opportunities. For her own reasons, this was not a route she was keen to take. Hence there was a crossroads of choice. *Did I keep this talented person to develop my still embryonic team, knowing her skills were underused, or did I support her to find opportunities beyond Howe Dell?* The decision was instant: she deserved the chance to do so much more than I could offer – I had a deficit budget, falling numbers and hence School-based options were minimal. I felt if I did this in the short term, opportunities may arise for us to work together in the future. Therefore, we worked together to explore options beyond the School, resulting in Nina working initially part-time but eventually full-time with the foster care team.

This was not the end of our story, as Nina kept in touch, not just out of nostalgia or friendship, but because she had seen change that was rapid at Howe Dell and she believed those changes were making an impact. She was a regular visitor to our website, to follow our progress!

When I advertised for a Children's Centre Manager, Nina contacted me and I said I felt she was not ready for that level of strategic responsibility: a frankness and honesty she valued. There is, I believe, no point, when asked directly, in encouraging someone to apply for a position when you know the person specification does not make this viable or a professional development opportunity.

However, six months later, having trialled an After School Club and Breakfast Club for six weeks through offering overtime for teaching assistants, to ensure viability and quality, Nina successfully applied for a newly created extended services coordinator position. The job description is available on the companion website. This has grown beyond belief! Nina not only provides training for the After School Club and Breakfast Club, but manages budgets and co-ordinates family learning, clubs and holiday play schemes on site. She has represented me at extended Schools consortium, previously only attended by Heads. She is also becoming tenacious in seeking grants and building links with our local community.

Mentoring is a key to modelling rapid growth and change

Initially, Nina required lots of support, mostly to reaffirm what she was doing and for us to grow the next chapter together. This certainly was not due to insecurity on her part, but the fact that we were forging something new and untested, so close communication was needed. Moreover, barriers to her success were largely from other professionals beyond Howe Dell, accepting Nina as my representative.

Within a term, the management of the provision on site was tighter, with organized, transparent systems in place. Within a year, waste of food had been reduced and children had a greater voice in determining menus and play provision. Clubs co-ordinated by Nina, whether by School staff, parents or outside agencies, were efficiently managed. Initially, there was close mentoring of Nina's role from me, but within months it became clear that she was beginning to lead in her own right and, as a result, I did not spread myself too thinly in covering this area of development. Proof of our success was evident in waiting lists for After School and Breakfast clubs and within two years, our play schemes in School holidays were also oversubscribed, largely due to word of mouth. The constant positive feedback was regularly posted on our website and celebrated in our weekly

Family Learning celebration evening, showing parents and proud children, celebrating their new found qualifications, Autumn 2010.

newsletter; again, examples of evaluation forms are available via the companion website.

Her leadership was demonstrated by her managing of teams, dealing with confrontation (mostly due to bad debts from parents) and the growth of viable businesses, all thoroughly evaluated. Some of the evaluations of projects introduced by Nina are available via our School website. The empowerment of this young leader has impacted on her personal leadership style and has made her a role model for her peers. As provision has grown, teaching assistants initially employed as play leaders in Breakfast/ After School clubs are now managers. Most recently, family learning, initially through craft activities, as a non-threatening way forward, now has eleven families working on maths programmes, with ICT and Literacy courses to follow. The opportunities are endless and exciting!

Learning beyond a case study – to move the team forward

What I have learnt most from Nina is that leadership growth cannot be forced and is not always linear. Moreover, support might need to be creative, to integrate a new role and personality into a ready-formed leadership team, but to also provide training to meet everyone's needs. Hence, I invited an outside trainer to support all members of the leadership team on training that we called 'Handling Hot Potatoes'. This had relevance to all members of the team. By asking members to evaluate easy and more difficult parts of their role, a common issue arose which involved the occasional, but inevitable, confrontation with the public. A blank version of this is available via the companion website, whilst a completed grid is included here, showing how I offered my own experience to encourage other team members to share and to trust one another.

'Handling Hot Potatoes': Leadership Day
The Whalley-Whitaker leadership contract: a chance to review the challenges of leadership.

Hard task **Happy process** Appraisal for a member of staff when both leader and staff member know there are difficult issues to resolve, yet from active listening and clear target-setting, also aware that staff is supported in developing skills. Outcome positive for both parties.	**Hard task** **Horrid process** Following a whistle-blowing incident, dealing with the 'fallout', which can run the risk of dividing staff loyalties.
Easy task **Happy process** Interviewing a member of the team who has been studying to level 4 to extend skills and knowledge. You interview them and they get the job.	**Easy task** **Horrid process** Disciplining a member of staff about timekeeping when they have been consistently late.

I used an example from my role to give colleagues a chance to reflect on their own situation before the day, and asked them to bring a scenario they were happy to share with a colleague. Giving choices along the way, trying a new and risky training strategy, is important, so long as the overall objective is met!

Further training tools to develop empathy between members of the growing leadership team could include a light hearted review of stereotypes. As by now, every department was represented via a leadership team line manager, the traditional roles were unpicked. For example, the expectations of a caretaker were explored and the competencies of Chris our Facilities Manager were then collated, not by him or me, but by colleagues. Sometimes this was a list of skills, but occasionally there were questions asked and clarification was achieved. It was crucial to sustainability of leadership, and possibly my sanity, that Chris's role took the pressures of site, premises and risk assessments off me. What it also required was credibility from other colleagues with more traditional management roles. Strategically, this was an expensive appointment and therefore meant my own salary scale was put on hold to begin with, despite ever increasing responsibility, but Chris's role, above all others, has helped me regain that life–work balance.

In creating a School of the future, this appointment was essential in demonstrating how to do things differently, to make staffing work for the organization, rather than just following what others have done before. Advice regarding pay scale and job description was on hand from Human Resources, but at the end of the day, Heads do have the power to create a team to meet needs and more should be brave enough to do so.

Likewise, to show graphically the stress points across the year for each department, a visual display was created to highlight where more than one area of Howe Dell might be under great strain at any time. Again I used an example for my role before asking staff to create their own.

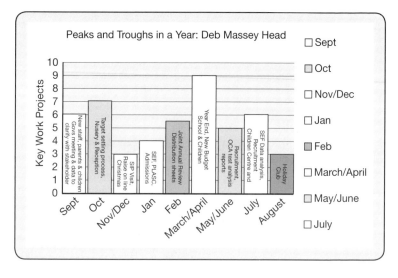

Whilst some stressful times in the year are fixed, such as financial year end or testing in May, others can be rearranged to spread the load and develop support and empathy. For example, Children's Centre staff no longer rely heavily on the School administration team on the first week of term; Day Care do their own banking in the School holidays; whilst clubs and lettings start the second week of each term, to provide some time to iron out last minute problems. It is common sense, but raises understanding between different groups and provides support where it is needed most. Moreover, through the success of our weekly short leadership team meetings, communication has improved and no longer uses me as the channel for all knowledge! Open evenings and community events are planned alongside the School diary and there has been a notable shift in groups from different areas of the organization supporting each other's out-of-hours projects. The combined stress across the site was immediately diminished and the opportunities to work across departments were strengthened.

How to link departments beyond the voice of the leadership team

By having members of a team complete dual roles across the whole organization, it enabled the vision of working as a whole site multi-agency provider for children and their families to be embedded quickly and with depth.

In every organization, there are **cornerstones**: in ours, these are all members of the leadership team. However, as we grew to meet the integrated services, education and extended schools agendas at Howe Dell, there needed to be **keystones** to strengthen this. This forged links strongly between colleagues who would not otherwise have worked together.

Without keystone roles, our hub School and Children Centre would not run with a shared vision and ethos.

By 2010, these roles had changed again, but that is the nature of good change management: no one knows all the answers, but with consultation, a greater variety of solutions are available, upon which to build. Please refer to the companion website for a diagram of what these keystone roles entailed.

The journal entry below shows how one needs to listen to what staff require for professional development: it's not always well timed, but can be strengthening for an organization. This was the case when my Deputy Day Care Manager came and told me she wanted to specialize in Children's Centre provision: she was an invaluable keystone worker and we had only been open for three months! I was keen to keep her, but equally keen to ensure her skills were best used. Perhaps what this entry also demonstrates is that Alison felt comfortable coming to talk through how she felt, the main reason why we are still working together at Howe Dell today. Journalling is a powerful tool to reflect on self-performance and prioritize when at times there is a danger of overload. It is also a tool to explore empathy with the perspective of another colleague and to provide planning and thinking time prior to challenging situations.

---

23 January 2008

BUILDING ON STRENGTHS NOT BUREAUCRACY

My heart initially sank ... so much for consolidation, so much for distributive leadership ... this team member was invaluable and retention was a priority.

Rather than jump in with immediate solutions, I resisted the temptation to sort as a 'quick fix' ... Instead, I thanked Alison for her honesty and asked if I could have some time to think about ways forward. I also asked her to do the same and to meet again, at a mutually convenient time the following day. We had both had a chance to reflect and the dialogue was positive. I had considered the strengths of what was being achieved in the afternoon sessions for young families – reliant on Alison's skills – and used that as the basis for planning. She did have to apply for a position which was already advertised for a nursery early years qualified practitioner and covered for teacher planning time in Reception Class as part of her new role, to make this financially viable and acceptable to both parties.

Ironically, two years later this colleague's role has changed again, as she embarked upon a Foundation Degree and is an outreach worker in our Children's Centre.

Back to Nina's Story

Nina is now working full-time rather than term-time only, and she continues to effortlessly manage extended services. Her excellent communication skills and credibility with the children have ensured she has organized whole-site projects, including Investors in People Gold Accreditation (see the Howe Dell website for more details on this). She has in fact mentored another new member of the leadership team, hence that journey to sustainable and distributive leadership continues.

We are a long way from the old site and that angry young boy, but our shared vision remains true to that early scenario. Nina is utterly committed to Every Child Matters, is a key professional on our leadership team, and a member of staff in whom I have complete faith. This is evident not only in how she interacts with the children, but how she supports some of our most vulnerable parents and how articulately she cascades our message to the wider community.

Key points for consideration

◆ The challenge is to encourage ongoing professional development: Nina's role was created out of school need, not through a traditional job description. It is always worth considering *'What do I need?'* rather than appointing what you have had before. This then becomes skill-based and considers whole team areas of strength and needs for development.

◆ If you have an idea, but are unsure of its viability, use a pilot project! The After School Club trial period meant no new contracts were needed and a six week project gave us a chance to learn from mistakes and include the voice of stakeholders (pupils and parents) to shape provision. By using staff already employed and advertising it as a pilot project, and therefore paying the additional hours worked as overtime, you have long enough to work through teething problems, a good opportunity to evaluate and reshape provision, as we did for our After School Club, gauge stakeholders' views and yet not commit to longer-term engagement until you are certain that it is appropriate to do so.

◆ Use midday supervisors or teaching assistants to pilot extended services provision. This way the personnel are already known to the School, can be paid overtime for cover and, if interested and if it becomes a permanent part of the School provision, they can apply through the usual means. Be sure to have an advertisement external to the School as well as internally to comply with the Equal Opportunities legislation.

◆ Play leaders are paid on the advice of Hertfordshire County Council at midday supervisor pay levels. However, to motivate teaching assistants, all were paid at an average teaching assistant rate, with a manager at a higher rate still. This encouraged highly experienced staff, often already with teaching assistant responsibility, to apply, and raised the status of this work. This will need to be worked into the costings, be transparent in charging and remissions and should be with the agreement from your Governing Body.

◆ When considering nationally accredited programmes such as

Quality Marks, try to include extended services in the process for cross-departmental learning. As a result of this process, all children in extended provision, such as an After School or Breakfast club, are assessed through their play. This uses the same criteria applied to Foundation Stage assessment and informs learning journals collated by Reception Class teachers. Looking at the Environmental Review for Early Years, the After School and Breakfast clubs were also assessed. It can bring unity to School and extended services and celebrates whole site excellence as well as the child in his or her entirety.

◆ Give different groups the chance to voice their differences and their shared agendas. By using different learning styles you are likely to reach more people – see the training tools from the Visual Peaks and Troughs graphical interpretation, and the 'Handling Hot Potatoes' grid which can be found on the companion website. It also gives a leader the chance to revisit the same ground but also reach more members of the team.

◆ Be aware, whatever the tool you use, some members of your team will be more vocal as to their role and needs. You could easily reinforce stereotypes, without appropriate questioning to make the playing field level. For example: 'We all know Year 6 testing is important, but Penny (Children's Centre Manager), can you clarify for all of us what an annual conversation for Children Centre is …?' So it is very similar to a joint annual review for the School.' Thus you will raise the profile of the younger sibling organization in terms of credibility, and yet, reaffirm common ground.

◆ Likewise, a Quality Mark for Children younger than 5 has been enriched in terms of staff training, ongoing provision and whole-site shared vision via the Quality Mark Scheme. We fought to be evaluated across Day Care, Children's Centre, Foundation Stage 0–5 and Extended Services: shape this to meet the needs of your organization and include voluntary or outreach work as appropriate.

◆ Every organization has capacity for 'Keystone Workers'. Determine where yours are and celebrate their importance via whole site training. We now have Trios emerging, led by a member of the leadership team and responsible for liaising once a term with representatives from School, Day Care and extended services, to enable whole site development on sustainable education, creativity, inclusion, and technology.

◆ Apply for grants – especially via local councils. Nina has also utilized the Disadvantage Grant creatively in consultation with me to reach not just free school meal children, but those just above the poverty line for whom child care or resources to enable sport or the arts to be accessed has been life changing. At a time of recession, many pots of money may go, but Grants for Schools have some up-to-date links.

◆ Try www.grants4schools.info as a starting point.

3

Children As Leaders: Growing Citizens for a Stronger World in the Future

It is my first day at Howe Dell and after an assembly's attempt to motivate a group of very passive or disengaged Year 5 and 6, the PowerPoint ended with a promise of 'Feeling Good Week' being booked within the first half-term and including Bollywood dance and raft building. As the children left the hall I was approached by a boy who looked exhausted at the prospect of another day in School. 'When are we getting wet?' he asked in a disinterested, laborious manner. This question was then followed by a look which showed a savvy intelligence – 'And 'ow much is it?'

Further dialogue revealed this was Johnnie. He was in Year 6 and he liked the sound of the raft building. Ironically at a time of below 90 per cent attendance, I had not told the children the day this adventure would take place, but reassured Johnnie it was free of charge… 'You see, I don't come every day, but I don't wanna miss that,' was his explanation.

Three cheers for pupil voice: Johnnie joined my Children's Council. He was still often late, but his attendance improved dramatically!

The point about pupil voice is that it trips off the adult tongue like 'beans on toast' or 'because I said so …' Too often it is a phrase, a tick in the box, a paragraph in the self-evaluation documents. For pupil voice to have any impact at all, it needs to have relevance to the children's needs and interests. Furthermore, when they have said something, how do they know they have been heard? What impact do their ideas have on the day-to-day and the longer-term vision of a school?

Are we nearly there yet?

When I was recently invited to Westminster following an interview regarding my view on new school buildings, I said I could only attend if some of my 'clients' came with me. There was a moment's pause and a clearing of throat when I explained this meant some children attending too. If we are not consulting children on what is relevant and valued in school design, then surely, we really have lost our way!

As it happened, three children *did* attend, all Year 6 and not all confident public speakers; indeed, rather nervous at the prospect of getting on a Tube and train, with a Head notorious for getting lost in the most unlikeliest of places! (The previous year, having taken a group of Year 6 pupils representing our Children's Council to Hemel Hempstead, a child phoned the School to announce we would be too late on our return to meet the School bus, 'because Mrs Massey went the wrong way on the motorway'!)

Flo' came with an earnest expression and a note book, which she explained was 'to write down anything important that anyone says, so that I can report back to School what this was all about'. Jake was more interested in collecting second-hand newspapers on the train and was somewhat daunted by the rush hour crowds at Kings Cross. Scarlett chatted incessantly about her family, especially older brother Sid, who had advised her to 'enjoy every minute, as you don't realize how great these opportunities are until you leave Howe Dell'. (Sid had been one of three children from Howe Dell, the only state primary school, to attend the return home of the Royal Anglian Regiment from Iraq the previous year. He and two other Children's Council representatives charmed their way to the front and I stood looking on with pride as they mingled with the great and the good, including interviewing county councillors, veterans and relatives.)

Out of the mouths of babes: find opportunities to listen to what they are really saying

At Westminster, one of the children declared they had never been to London, so a hasty tour was undertaken of Horse Guards' Parade,

Sid with classmates Cheslea and Josh, photographing and reporting upon the return of the Royal Anglian Regiment from Iraq. Their report and photographs became a PowerPoint reported to the wider School community.

the Cenotaph, 10 Downing Street and Trafalgar Square – with hot chocolate along the way. It was a rare moment for me to listen to these wonderful children chat about holidays, families, hopes and dreams for the future, whilst they gawped and pointed at horses in livery, Churchill's statue and the armed police. They were incredibly aware of adult world issues such as family, education, the pros and cons of their home town. They were certainly less naïve than perhaps I had presumed, about life chances, drugs and the challenges to overcome, in their bid to be successful adults.

On arrival at the Houses of Parliament all three became very quiet, rather overawed to the point that when a charming police officer declared smiling teachers were most welcome, but it is written in the law of the land that children have to pay £5 to come in, they looked panic stricken!

Yet as we arrived at the Terrace Pavilion and met the then Minister for State Schools and others, I watched the children relax more and begin to enjoy the occasion. They were asked their views on sustainability and suggestions for future schools. They were so obviously proud of their own school, but also able to grapple with more objective issues. 'You see,' said Scarlett, 'what you should do is build these new schools for the youngest children, because they have parents coming into the school more. Children's Centres could help parents with looking after babies and toddlers. If young children understood about the "eco" ideas behind the buildings, they'd tell the parents and that changes adult attitudes.'

It reminded me of a previous Year 6 pupil explaining to an ITN *News at Ten* reporter, 'It's harder for adults 'cos they've had bad habits for longer. But I tell my dad, "You don't need the car, you can walk to the shops!"' It really is that simple: at times children can voice the common sense answers that we adults appear to have forgotten!

Questions arising from engaging pupil voice

- ◆ How do you make it meaningful and relevant to pupil interest?
- ◆ How do you fit in yet another priority in an already overcrowded timetable?
- ◆ How can the wider community engage with this work?
- ◆ Where does it have impact?

ICT: a powerful tool

The children at Westminster explained about the work they were doing in school, how technology, such as blogging and sharing PowerPoint presentations in assembly or via our website, informed a wider audience of their views. The internet really can bring the world to the classroom and our doubling the national average results this year in writing were certainly partly due to creative communication, using this technology, coupled with Simon's and Ginny's outstanding teaching. They proudly explained their ICT project on global warming had won a national competition which had resulted in them deciding as a class that the £500 prize should go towards a sensory garden, so that children who were visually impaired could get as much out of the school grounds development as they did. Ironically, Simon took that to Europe and Cape Town for a Global Innovative Teaching Award. It used technology which can be accessible to 5-year-olds and whilst the movies were great, the opportunity for independent research, collaboration and presenting to one another was empowering and could be replicated.

Likewise, with younger children in Year 2, Sarah, a teacher studying for her MA, prepared for a staff meeting by asking the children in her class what creativity was. The results were typed into Microsoft's

Wordle and the following summary was presented to the whole staff. Later, this was used as the stimulus behind a wider debate which shaped the School Development Plan. The PowerPoints to prompt wider discussion on creativity are available for use on the School website, as is the whole School development of this Wordle.

http://www.wordle.net/

Other means of using ICT to engage pupil voice might be:

◆ Use Nintendo DS to record voices and views, to later summarize or report. Tape recorders are great, but many children have these hand-held games consoles, so why not use them to 'spice up some speaking and listening' with some 'street cred'?

◆ Set up a group elsewhere in the School with a web cam to have a safe video conference. This might involve role play, giving children the 'mantle of expert' to empower views. Simon's recent plan extended this to engage with a United Nations conference. The children and staff accept that technology can sometimes inhibit quality of involvement as well as empower, but surely that is all part of the learning process? Simon's experience with such projects ensured that all safety elements were relayed to me, governors and parents prior to the tasks taking place.

◆ Have a class blog, open for a set period of time and managed by the class teacher. This needs to be checked for E- safety, but such projects have inspired the writer and speaker in our Year 6, with dramatic results. This also gives the participant reflection time prior to responding.

◆ Give children digital cameras and include them on learning walks with staff around the School. The angle of the photographs gave a new perspective to adults. Again, their findings were reported to governors and School, whilst video of the children's discussions were an invaluable insight. For example, a boy of 8 was able to explain that a particular display was very creative as it had a range of different work, and children had been given the freedom to make choices. Another child explained that a Maths lesson was creative in its use of technology, encouraging skill practice in a motivational way, again giving children a range of strategies to use.

Give the children real dilemma-based purposes for debate

It was on this Westminster occasion that I was able to stand back and watch pupil power command attention from some of the key people who would be shaping education and school buildings, possibly for

Flo, Scarlett and Jake representing the UK's Pupil Voice at Westminster, November 2009. Accompanied by a headteacher who was only there to make up the numbers!

years to come. The children explained that when researched more thoroughly, they did not have the funds for the sensory garden, so instead a chicken house was bought and we now boast four chickens on site. Even this decision was not straightforward and involved the Children's Council writing to the Governing Body and a change of policy being agreed as a result. Despite the chickens not arriving until after Year 6 left in the summer term, many have returned to check that their money was well spent! The fact that the project had obstacles was important in the learning process, as it meant tough decisions needed to be made and compromises agreed.

Prior to leaving, Flo' said, 'I was a bit nervous about the networking, but when people realized what we were saying was important, we didn't have to circulate, they queued to listen to us.' 'Yes,' added Jake, 'but we do need business cards!'

How much peer credibility can a pupil council have?

When asked 'What do children think of the impact of Children's Council?' the results below show an openness and high expectation resulting from Children's Council engagement. There is a PowerPoint to prompt debate from pupils which can be adapted by any school, but the following results from Howe Dell show clarity of understanding, on which we have built.

What does the Children's Council do?	What else COULD it do?
Meet with Mrs Massey regularly – listen to our comments and report back ideas about the School.	Speak to important people like governors more often.
Raise money for equipment and furniture.	Talk about improvements to the School/what it needs.
Make posters and discuss Wonder Days.	Continue to raise money.
	More events.
Do some of the Newsletters.	Doughnuts to be returned to lunch menu.

What does the Children's Council do?	What else COULD it do?
Do charity events, e.g. sorted shoes for *Blue Peter* appeal. Organize a non-uniform day.	Milkshakes for lunch. Plant a new Wellentonia tree.
They raise money for School trips.	Check suggestion box weekly.
Organize fairs and events. Represent the School at events.	Organize more football and basketball matches.
Take notes in assembly, to add to newsletter or website.	
Show parents and other important guests around our School.	
Children's Council is most of Year 6; anyone who wants to be on it can be, so long as their behaviour is good.	
If being bullied, go to Children's Council.	

Assembly: the perfect opportunity: don't waste it!

Whether whole school, large group or class based, these at worst are passive opportunities for the many to be spoken to at length by the few and usually those speakers are adults! At best, these can be opportunities to open debate, raise issues, celebrate individuals and groups, inspire and extend.

♦ Give the children a chance to contribute! Short, snappy chances to talk to people near them, then draw back to a more formal summary of volunteers' contributions. Have a clear means of drawing the children back to you (counting back from five, raised hand, clapping rhythm: it doesn't matter what strategy, so long as it is consistent across the School for maximum impact). We use counting back from five, with the disclaimer that we never need to go below four, as children are so well mannered at Howe Dell. This reinforcement of high expectation works and the registered Ofsted inspector admitted she had never achieved that in her own school!

◆ Children's Council can make notes on key assembly themes – for us the reasons for children achieving 'Beacon Pupil' for their class is written up by the Children's Council and added to the weekly newsletter. Give a child with a short concentration span a note pad and pen and you have engaged more of that child than you would if you expected him or her to sit passively for 20 minutes!

◆ At times, provide all children with post-its or scatter the group with Children's Council representatives to annotate discussions. One successful strategy led by our Deputy was with Key Stage 2: this has been used as a way of extending self-evaluation, enhancing an entrance hall display, or spreading the message via laminated post-its on key doors through the School:

✓ 'What goals will I set myself this term?'
✓ 'Where in the World has my family lived?'
✓ 'What I love about Maths.'

◆ Split the School into smaller mixed-age groups to discuss key issues on school improvement, which can then shape School Development Plans. Our version is called Pupil Forum and the key questions are circulated a week prior to the event to teachers to set up on interactive whiteboards. Adults act as scribes whilst the debate is led by Children's Council representatives. Examples of this are on the companion website, exploring eco aspirations and creativity. A hands up survey at the end gives a clear message about what pupil voice is saying, as here when asked which of the traditionally arts based subjects, the children preferred:

What we enjoy most	No. of votes
Art	80
Music	42
Drama	17
D.T.	35
Dance	30

Pupil voice can be articulated using senses beyond speech

Recently, this has involved drawing as a collaborative task, to create flags to celebrate what the School and Children's Centre stands for, or rain forest role play to encourage empathy with global issues. Copies of PowerPoints to be adapted for similar projects are available via the companion website. Results collated by the Children's Council on which group earned the most votes for their arguments are shown here. What was striking was that whilst we have chosen to employ this approach to Year 1 and above due to the formality and timescale, when there was a role play situation such as the rain forest debate, the youngest children were the most creative thinkers. As suggested regarding staff development, perhaps this reiterates a need to guard against stereotypical misconceptions and give brave ideas a chance with our children as the leaders!

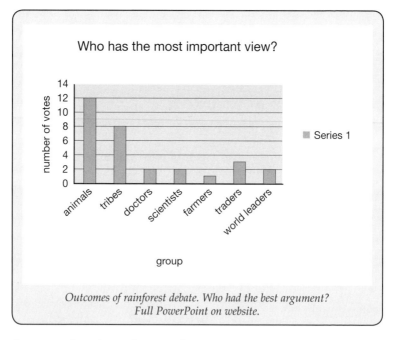

Outcomes of rainforest debate. Who had the best argument?
Full PowerPoint on website.

An example of pupil voice having impact was when children responded that they spoke to governors least. When reported back to the full Governing Body, it was patiently explained 'It's because we don't know who you are.'

Which adults?	How many votes?
Teachers	79
Dinner staff, office or TA team	46
Governors	13
Parents	122

An extract from a Children's Council presentation.

Since then governor link visits include pupil engagement and a number of governors have committed to regular visits to School, to forge strong relationships with key pupils. This has transformed the way in which governors have planned interaction with pupils and at least one full Governing Body a term out of two always starts with a group of children presenting a project or piece of research, taking questions from the floor. Initially, this needs coaching, but very quickly the children collate the information and draft the PowerPoint – the first time I see it is when it goes live. This has also demonstrated the impact of pupil voice, with governor engagement changing quickly in response to this feedback. This takes trust and a scaffold of support, which is eventually surplus to requirements.

Introduce a suggestion box to encourage ad hoc responses from pupils beyond the formal opportunities, for seeking their views

◆ This is in the main entrance and all ideas can be published via the newsletter alongside a response from the School and a member of staff/governors or pupil group to action the response. This is fed back each term and all suggestions are posted on our website, to make it manageable.

◆ The occasional (two in eight years!) nasty anonymous letter creeps in – but publish that, too, responding, 'I don't know who you are, but you are clearly very cross – come and chat to me!' This shows we are professionals who listen, but puts the anonymous input into context!

◆ It is important this isn't seen as a way that everything is solved but consideration of every idea is really encouraging inclusivity.

Use the community to enrich and extend opportunities to discuss with a wider range of adults

◆ From knocking on doors with Harvest goodies to reminding neighbours of our fete and apologizing for any inconvenience due to noise or congestion – face-to-face contact really has impact.

◆ One example was when in a Harvest delivery a local elderly resident asked, 'What will your School and Children's Centre do for the likes of us?' A child responded, 'Well what would you like it to do?' As a result the Silver Surfers' ICT Club was born! (The title was borrowed from a similar project in a local secondary school).

◆ Local businesses often have mission statements which encourage community cohesion. Our visit to the water board resulted in a return visit by our pupils in Year 5 who evaluated the company's eco credentials and set six months targets ... and they returned to establish whether these targets have been met. The outcome for Howe Dell was volunteers arriving to create our vegetable garden.

◆ Children in School uniform attending the supermarket on the last day of an educational scheme seeking unwanted vouchers with a member of staff pays dividends, as does a visit with some persuasive children to local providers of raffle prizes!

◆ Our Children's Council is purely Year 6 as it is easier for timetabling and extends the level of debate and dialogue with increased opportunities within the curriculum, e.g. data analysis of Pupil Forum in Year 6 Maths lessons. However, it grew from necessity, referring back to Johnnie, a disaffected Year 6 lad who knew the promise of a new school would not be in his time. Therefore, by including Year 6 in an 'all welcome' culture, engagement was encouraged. Those who were in previous year groups were then invited back for our Royal visit and official opening. Of 45 invited, 23 attended in a rainbow of local secondary uniforms.

ECO Squad, Green Beans, Eco Warriors ... What is the name of YOUR sustainability group?

Eco Squad has representatives from *every* class, from Reception Class to Year 6. As a result, these are voted in with ever increasing pupil-led independent efforts, age and stage dependent. In Reception, it is still usual for the teacher to choose representatives who enjoy learning outdoors; in Key Stage 1 there is consideration by adults as to who has aptitude and interest in the world at large; whilst in Key Stage 2, a full ballot following presentations takes place. However, in an early meeting, the children were able to articulate the following, thus showing strength of belief and understanding that reaffirms that children have plenty to say, if only we take time to listen.

When asked, Eco Squad recommended:

◆ *Save more electricity.*
◆ *Look after school grounds.*
◆ *Use both sides of the paper!*
◆ *Plant our own fruit trees.*
◆ *Have more outside bins.*
◆ *Introduce Litter Pickers!*
◆ *Introduce bird feeders.*
◆ *Water butt for collecting rainwater to use in the garden.*
◆ *Have lessons to learn how to ride bikes safely.*

All of this is now in place ... and so much more!

Key points for consideration

◆ Scaffold speaking and listening opportunities in class: in the early days, I asked for these to be highlighted in blue in planning, so that the level of focus was clear from a monitoring point of view.
◆ Make assemblies active and engage pupil voice within them, but record this using the pupils as note takers.
◆ Use post-its or big paper to ensure inclusion of as many views as possible.
◆ Art and role play can capture views beyond what especially younger children can record in writing or formal speech.
◆ Make the focus of debate relevant to the children and give feedback so that they know their voices may be heard.
◆ Pupil Forum is a norm at Howe Dell, but took planning and good communication between adults so that the theme was circulated in advance. The early events especially needed to be led by the senior leadership team to give it prestige.
◆ Forge links with your local neighbours: it pays back tenfold and brings the enterprise of the real world into the classroom.
◆ Use ICT to open doors for communication. Blogging has had a dramatic impact on reluctant writers who now engage in debate beyond school hours. Next mission – radio station!

4

I Trust You to Make that Decision: Distributing Leadership and Feeding the Souls of Staff as well as Pupils

Change was rapid when I began at Howe Dell, energy levels within the staff and pupil sectors visibly rose, yet it came at a price. I was leading six subject areas, had no deputy and some temporary staff. This leadership was necessary in the short term as I had no choice, but long term it simply wasn't sustainable – nor healthy.

I look back at that first half-term and it seems like a different world. On a daily basis, behaviour management, subject leadership, new build, curriculum projects, leading the content of every staff meeting … the list was endless and was totally dependent upon a very directive style.

However, by the October half-term, not only children but the parents and indeed many staff were buzzing with the success of our 'Feeling Good Week'. What was this magical Feeling Good Week? It was an off-curriculum themed week, encouraging children to have opportunities to try new skills and experiences. The ethos was beginning to change and so too could my role.

During that week, staff who had been reluctant to join in the various activities, from Bollywood dancing to raft building and kayaking, had been encouraged to take risks in their teaching, without the confines of a prescriptive curriculum. Unsurprisingly, new evidence of the creativity and skills and interests of staff was beginning to impact upon the learning. An example of this was when Sara had her Year 6 pupils draw around each other in positions linked to the Bollywood dance, whilst Indian music played. As these figures were painted and draped in exotically coloured fabric, it was clear that the children lacked the skill to do this task at a high level and the experience to work collaboratively. But she persevered with the glue and the paint, she encouraged the children to spread out into the hall and main entrance and the result was that collaboration was beginning to emerge – and there were no dramatic behaviour issues for her, or me, to deal with, which was a first! (To put this into context, the small class of 23 Year 6 pupils had been divided across mixed-age groups for the dance workshops, due to concerns that the boys' behaviour might impact negatively on the sessions.)

When a vacancy arises, see this as a chance to appoint what you haven't had, rather than replace like with like

Sara was newly appointed by me and believed totally in what I was aiming to do, but on a day-to-day basis had the frustration of being an excellent teacher with what were disengaged Year 6 pupils. They were well below their expected levels of attainment, with passive girls and some boys with very challenging behaviour. Her skills in the creative curriculum and her passion for learning were clear. She was appointed as Music subject leader, but was later on our leadership team for creativity. Whilst we worked as a comedic double act for 'singing assemblies', the quality of the sound and engagement of the children increased. However, it was Sara who introduced the choir to its first success.

Our Chair of Governors led an event in the autumn term called 'Songs of Praise' at the local church, for surrounding schools (primary and secondary) to contribute solo pieces and sing ensemble. He explained that at Howe Dell, only five or six children attended. Sara took up the gauntlet and avidly sold the choir and this opportunity, not just to the children but also to the parents. She and other teachers emptied lost property for our then yellow sweatshirts, to be washed and pressed, so that the 32 children who attended wore a uniform – and they not only matched, they simply shone! There were more Howe Dell children and parents there, not to mention staff, than from any other school: a proud moment for all.

The fact that Sara had been given the opportunity to lead this meant she did so with enthusiasm, but she also empowered children to do the same, as our School song included solos not only from girls but also a boy! This raised profile for music moved on at a pace and children contributed to a town carol service, a local schools concert at the university and, began planning for a performance at the Royal Albert Hall, all before Christmas 2005. Sara has now moved on to train as an art therapist, but her legacy for making creativity accessible to all remains.

Royal Albert Hall, 2010: Sara's legacy continues. This event was later modified by the new Music Subject Leader and Deputy Head, to ensure disruption to learning beyond Music was minimized. Hence, it is now recognized as a year group rather than a choir project.

A class teacher role does not need to evolve to traditional management positions

Sara's responsibility evolved from Year 6 teacher to Foundation Stage leader when we moved to the new site at the Runway. She was also awarded a Teaching and Learning Reward, which replaced the previous management points, not for a static subject but for a theme: creativity. Ironically, her love had always been Early Years, but I told her honestly at interview that the job available was for Year 6, but promised that her professional needs and interests would be developed. She jokingly reports to this day how it was all part of the 'good professional development' I had promised her.

This was first mentioned on a day when the lesson observation outcome was still only satisfactory, and she was tearful with frustration. It was not due to her teaching, which was excellent, but due to the pace and engagement of the learners, who had a history of loving school but finding 'learning an inconvenience of childhood'.

However, when Sara was appointed Foundation Stage leader, she attended planning meetings with the architects and it was her who chose resources for the Foundation Stage, including outdoor play equipment costing in the region of £30,000–£40,000. She was the working expert: I questioned her choices, listened to her views and went with her recommendations. This was invaluable for outdoor learning advice from Foundation Stage to Year 6: she had earned her spurs.

Questions emerging from a time of change and innovation

When a new leader arrives, so too do a storm of new ideas: what about those staff who are still loyal to a previous regime? How do you engage an open dialogue to ensure a shared understanding of priorities and next steps? How can you ensure there isn't a rift between 'inherited and chosen' staff?

Tried and tested suggested ways forward

◆ Use a training day, which gives you a chance to articulate the vision, but in a non threatening, inclusive way. I chose a 'Healthy Schools' theme, encouraging staff to give positive examples of what is already in place, then managing the suggestions for next steps. Using this directive style ensures that no one sabotages the discussion and the previous work of the School is given some credibility.

◆ Lace the hard messages with strong emotive suggestions for the children. For example, I reiterated, quoting from some of the staff contributions, how we are all here with a common focus, therefore the appalling sickness record of staff needed to improve. This followed a suggestion that staff wellbeing ought to be part of all our performance management, in order to grow a healthy, positive working environment. By so doing, I was able to use NAPTA teaching assistant resources to encourage self-review prior to individual performance management (see www.napta.org.uk). The Staff Handbook, previously mentioned, also laid out without any frills the professional etiquette expected within my School. This brought rigour to the new systems being introduced, but also clarity to a school where there had been too many grey areas.

◆ The hardest thing is to accept that loyalties and indeed friendships will remain and not get into the position of competing for that loyalty nor undermining the previous regime. This was very difficult at times for me as some staff met socially with local retired colleagues, but by inviting these ex-members of staff to the first Christmas celebrations, there was an openness and warmth that was genuine. It sent a strong message that this was now a new chapter, but they were welcome. The previous Head was also offered an opportunity to attend the Royal opening of the new site some years later, and ex-parents, staff and governors have an open invitation to attend our monthly 'Visitors' Days'.

◆ If there is undermining of the new leadership by personalities from a previous era, to a certain extent you have to trust your staff to be adults, however hurtful it might be. I found that staff were far from naïve and worked out for themselves whether I lived up to what I said!

◆ Email is an excellent way of celebrating daily successes and raising questions to which people can respond. For us, this replaced memos, was far more sustainable and didn't make a mess of the staff notice boards, which could then be organized to display key information and documents of relevance. Photographs of key events, including staff socials and minutes of meetings being displayed publicly also aids communication and reaffirms a sense of shared purpose. A virtual learning platform can also do this in the longer term.

◆ Use of website, email or a central screen in the entrance to the School, or via PowerPoints in assemblies, to celebrate weekly achievements, really raises the expectations and engagement of school communities.

◆ A regular newsletter with a positive yet consistent tone is also invaluable: ours always begins with 'Highlight of the week has been …' and it really works in focusing on the positives – as well as being an excellent marketing tool. Many examples of this are available via the School website.

◆ Certainly, early on, I ensured that any other business to be discussed at staff meetings was brought to my attention prior to the meeting, for timing purposes, to avoid any unwelcome surprises and to ensure that these items came just before the end of the meeting so that a quick pace was maintained!

◆ Setting up a classroom for a key piece of learning is done naturally by any good teacher: likewise, where I sat in the staffroom and with whom, how groupwork would be organized, and at times the venue, were all planned in advance. Having a staff meeting in Sara's room reaffirmed her love of creativity and credibility with her peers. It also gave me a chance to suggest learning walks on a term basis for us to see each other's areas and celebrate new initiatives. (For the disengaged, this is a key moment to 'raise their game' or for leaders to follow up, as appropriate.)

♦ If you are introducing new or unfamiliar roles and responsibilities, be very clear what these positions entail, in order to avoid preconceived ideas based on prior experience. Hence we reviewed our expectations of members of the leadership team's roles in the first year at the new site, to forge a greater understanding. This was later used as a training tool for the Children Centre and Day Care training day. The aims were to develop empathy and to review tasks set, for accountability and time management. This is best summarized in a question: *How can we support one another to build something even better?*

This was approached through an open and sometimes tongue-in-cheek look at where misunderstandings had taken place in the past! The full training PowerPoint to review the current position, and forge a way forward from a group of managers to a leadership team, is available via the website, as is the evaluation form used. The response was very positive and acknowledged a need to be off site, to share common ground and establish different perspectives too. Comments from feedback received include:

♦ Really positive day. Thank you. Great preparation for this evening's event [with a wider group of staff].
♦ Good day all round. Nice to meet up out of work and feel comfortable talking to each other.
♦ I do not look forward to days like this, but I found this informative and insightful, talking with and working with the members of our staff. A really good and worthwhile day.

What about those staff members who do not seize the limelight? How can their growth be nurtured?

A member of staff who was already working at Howe Dell on my arrival was Nikki, our ICT co-ordinator, now very much a subject leader in her own right. She was a quiet yet reflective member of staff who took a while to come forward with regard to subject leadership. I found this to be because previous staff had been reticent to try or even use (in some cases) ICT in their teaching or planning. However, it was clear on one-to-one discussions that Nikki had a strong understanding of what was required from a resources point of view, as well as being supportive of a progressive skill-based learning approach. She had also been involved in the eco curriculum mapping, so therefore had a clear understanding as to how ICT development ought to include this.

Unlike Sara's leadership opportunity, Nikki's was more gradual: personality and attributes beyond teaching and learning must shape how staff development is planned. However, in the next two years our ICT provision map, with advice from Hertfordshire County Council and resulting assessment shared as excellent practice, led to us having a virtual learning platform and a BECTA Quality Mark for ICT. Nikki has joined the leadership team to oversee Technology across School, Centre and Day Care. Her strength remains her listening skills, her gentle, non-threatening manner when introducing new initiatives to staff and parents and her management of our ICT technician's time. Moreover, she is a bridge builder and has immense patience! Her being a governor involved in the Health, Safety and Premises Committee also gives her credibility with governors and facilities staff at an operational level.

Growth must be with sustainability embedded in the vision, on order to retain healthy, positive staff

In Autumn 2005 we were a small School and not only did I have six subject areas but Sara and Nikki had two each: Music/SEN and ICT/RE respectively. Therefore it was essential through performance management and strategic planning that only one subject was the focus per term and that adequate non-contact time was provided for these leadership roles to be done well. This did have budget implications, but it was a priority to move the curriculum leadership swiftly to a shared responsibility. How can you introduce distributive leadership through curriculum development, without burning out staff, or to the detriment of their class-based commitments? This is a challenge for any Head, but when pushed, I always plan an extensive supply budget and, if necessary, reduce resources to be bought. Our greatest resource is always our staff. This is reinforced in our staff pledge. This was created as part of our training day, and gave opportunities to explore what we value and how we support one another, but there was also a chance for 'colonic irrigation': a chance to moan about what gets in the way! The examples below prove we have not built a Utopia yet; shared ownership for the day-to-day issues needs continual review:

◆ Community Hall – shared resource with timetabling and organizational strain.
◆ Plastic recycling – who does it and think before you put something in the bin!
◆ Dishwasher and staffroom cleanliness.

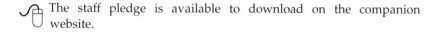 The staff pledge is available to download on the companion website.

Obstacles to battle ... or challenges to overcome: all a state of mind?

Staff sickness was a large leak on resources which needed plugging! This needed a strong directive style, which reaffirmed what the expectations of Howe Dell would be. It is essential that a new leader is able to articulate the vision: teams need to be led, before strengths within a team can be delegated wisely.

Hence, on my first day as Head – the INSET Day – I focused on the Healthy School award, with me setting out my stall by sharing my presentation to governors at interview to:

◆ motivate,
◆ ensure clarity,
◆ share the vision.

The morning then involved a series of workshops where mixed groups established what was already in place and possible next steps against the different headings. There was a real sense of purpose in the air and I actually had to interrupt groups to draw proceedings to a close for lunch! In the plenary, as we shared what was possible for our next year, I made it clear that:

◆ *Every* child matters at Howe Dell *every* day, but so too does *every* member of staff.

- Those with ongoing sickness-related absences would be referred promptly to Occupational Health for support and guidance, not just for the individual but also for the School.

- Training days given as a right at the beginning of the year would be redirected to cover sickness, if this became necessary.

- Supply was expensive and the staff were told it may mean, considering our current financial situation, that classes would have to double up, prior to insurance taking the cost of such absence, or teaching assistants would be responsible for the classes at a higher rate of pay. Drafting teaching assistants in from elsewhere in the School to cover short absences was necessary, but we needed to ensure their usual classes were still meeting legal ratio requirements, and that the teaching assistants demonstrated competence in this role.

- It was made very clear that any habitual or regular short absences would have a dramatic and inconvenient impact on us all, beyond the financial cost. This seems strong on reflection, but the culture towards sickness needed radical change.

- Staff sickness for the majority has never been an issue since then, and where it remained a concern, patterns (e.g. Mondays and Fridays!) were logged and procedures were brought into place.

- Likewise, for those who have been bereaved or needed long-term sick leave, flowers and contact were introduced to ensure that a member of staff knew that the support from colleagues was without question. It was the right of all, not the privilege of a few.

With the phrase 'I trust you to make that decision' comes responsibility on both sides and if we were to grow an outstanding school, professionalism had to run through the organization like the name of a seaside town through a stick of confectionery rock. This vision is reflected in our staff pledge but also the Wordle (Microsoft) which resulted from the leadership team articulating what they felt about their job. This began with a force field diagram, entitled 'May the Force Be with You', available on the website. Both positive and negative Wordles shared with the whole staff can give a visual image which may then be interpreted by a wider audience. Here, let's focus on the positive!

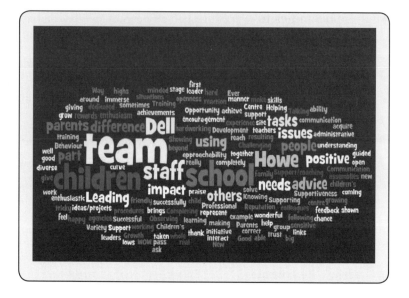

A light bulb moment!

It is during times of great change that leadership challenges can be so vast and all consuming that there is a need to consolidate, before realistic next steps can be established.

In my journal during the transition to the new site and during the next year, I was struck by the clarity emerging from a simple self-evaluation task. It began with a drawing depicting the emotional health of my setting and then a review of the bubbles and cartoons, to establish a way forward. By asking myself some basic questions, priorities became clear and manageable. Please refer to the companion website for the full evaluation evolving from this.

♦ What can I control?
♦ What can I influence?
♦ What can't I control?

'There is nothing more difficult to take in hand, more perilous to conduct, or more uncertain in its success, than to take the lead in the introduction of a new order of things.' Machiavelli (1513)

Find opportunities to celebrate the change in behaviour or attitude

◆ On a positive note, 'Smiley Days' have since been given as additional paid leave for individuals attending a family event or departments who have gone above and beyond the call of duty at a difficult time: trust is a symbiotic process, beneficial to leaders and those led.

◆ Likewise, after our community fete, we open later on the Monday to ensure the site is safe. This has had minimum challenge from parents, is agreed by the governors and published to parents nine months in advance. Queries were addressed through our Parent Voice Group, thus showing they had been considered, but recognizing staff wellbeing as something valued by all.

Grow the roles closest to that of Head to provide sustainability and extend leadership structure

As the team developed and were 'bought into the vision', there was time to consider growth and development as we moved from a small primary school to a two-form entry with Children's Centre and Day Care plus Extended Services. The leadership could not continue to be linear and a further increase in distributive leadership was necessary. This initially meant that our new Deputy, albeit a very good teacher, was new to a senior leadership role within our School and had to support me with day-to-day organization. As she also had a heavy class-teaching responsibility, this tended to be a management role to begin with, embedding the vision and curriculum at the old site, especially when I was involved in the new building project. Once we moved to the new site, Deputy non contact time was extended to support leadership in School and training was available, to extend skills. This later resulted in a review of staff structuring and recent extension of our Senior Leadership Team, as new challenges included possible succession leadership needing to be considered by governors and the Senior Leadership Team.

Delegation could only go so far, because Deputy's main responsibility was her Year 6 class and raising standards and progress rates for the children in her care. Recently, she has increased non-contact time, being four afternoons a week and two additional hours, so that she is still has overarching responsibility for her class, but no longer has Year 6. As a result, she is able to take a stronger leadership role in the organization of teaching assistants and interviewing midday supervisors. She also represents me as acting Head at times to parents and to governors through the Curriculum Committee and is due to coordinate link governor curriculum visits. The additional two hours also supported her as she embarked on NPQH training for an aspiring Head!

The first big change in role was when performance management of teaching assistants became the Deputy's responsibility and there needed to be a change in culture, so that staff and parents did not always expect me to be a first port of call. As we have grown further, however, teaching assistant line management and performance management has been referred to Key Stage leaders and the Deputy has more non-contact time for leadership and management to oversee student placements. Both she and our Children's Centre Manager have developed their understanding of leadership more fully by the professional development available via NPQH and NPQICL training respectively. This has given both individuals the knowledge to apply skills to a broader range of incidences including the more complex/ challenging scenarios such as complaints or community engagement. The result of this is that at times I can be a critical friend to them as leaders – we meet weekly to discuss key issues and projects – but there is a given acceptance that they are responsible for moving these issues forward. Without publicly receiving acknowledgement from the Head, the credibility of these two senior leaders is compromised. This became apparent when I interviewed our Children Centre Manager for a piece of research in April 2008; it was a chance for me to really reflect upon letting go of certain aspects of leadership, but doing so publicly in order to give her a chance to develop. If Rosenthal is to be believed, this is a very feminine leadership trait:

> ... integrated leadership ... is perhaps more common in the humble 'affairs of parents, teachers and peers'. In this sense, integrative leadership is about listening and engaging ... [It] also stresses empowerment of others, a feminist conceptualization of power as support and cooperation rather than domination.
> Cindy Simon Rosenthal, *Reviewing Women as Leaders*, 1998, p. 21

It was interesting how the difference in the interview with my Deputy was, due to the fact that by now this was an established relationship. Furthermore, due to the longevity of the Deputy's involvement with Howe Dell, compared to that of the new Children's Centre Manager, understanding of the overall vision, and therefore trust and autonomy, was heightened. Nevertheless, in creating a senior leadership team of three and establishing roles in a time of constant change is best clarified by demonstrating I have 2 deputies, one is curriculum focused, the other community driven. This heightened the profile of the Children's Centre Manager, who quickly became the main contact for community projects beyond the immediacy of the School. The thought of developing our provision without the strength and wisdom Penny brings to the leadership of Children Centre is now unimaginable: such is the impact of her developed role and whilst our leadership styles can be very different, the organisation is enriched by this partnership. Weekly meetings with each member of the senior leadership remains invaluable to coach, aid communication, focus on agendas specific to their role, rather than wider issues ... and sometimes to simply let off steam!

Green shoots beyond the leadership team

What became apparent as we moved to the Runway was how valuable members of staff were who had multiple contracts across the site and in different departments. These keystone workers, as already mentioned, were invaluable in cementing the vision but also communicating projects and priorities from one department to the next. Case Study 3 on the website demonstrates this through Jackie's story.

In the following chapters, growth utilizing the skills of other staff, governors and parents, as well as neighbours both local and global, will reiterate the value and strength of leading a sustainable school.

Not all projects work. Not all of these examples are transferable to other organizations, but the philosophy is. If you empower people to lead, they will do so, but at times the route may be different to that which you originally drafted. It might take longer than if the Head had done it alone, but the journey and outcome is richer for all that: and all live to tell the tale!

Key points for consideration

◆ When you have the chance to recruit, look for competencies and capabilities. Do you need to replace what has just left, or are there gaps in the whole team skill-base which could extend the shared leadership further?

- In supporting staff or governors to take on new leadership opportunities, scaffold it to ensure objectives are clear and that there is a transition period, where you are there to advise, annotate reports, model processes, just as we do for the children when teaching them to write.

- Ensure that if someone is given responsibility for a project or key development, it stays publicly as their 'baby' and that they are given the credibility by you as Head. If you are seen to trust them, so too will others.

- If it doesn't work out, sit down and unpick why and rebuild quickly. It's not about blame – it is about overcoming obstacles. It might be that the timing is not right or more planning time is needed – it does not automatically mean it is a bad idea!

- As well as modelling processes for your emergent leaders, consider the bigger picture. Most staff in this scenario when asked said that management of people was the hardest part; booking a counsellor to practise resolution of confrontational situations with the leadership team was invaluable. She has also been offered to a member of my leadership team to provide support when that person has had a difficult work-based issue to contend with. This is seen as a strength of wellbeing not a weakness.

- Use your county or borough support for occupational health, human resources and contractual advice: that is what they are there for.

- Track sickness patterns and act upon them quickly as an example of the rigour of the process behind the words of the vision.

- Remember, a good team needs a variety of personalities and skills. Look beyond those who might shout loudest to see who is most capable.

- Whatever else goes due to time constraints, communication with senior leaders, and others to whom you have delegated most, must remain a priority – otherwise, the shared ownership will be undermined and become silos working. The Head is the only person to oversee the whole site with the most objectivity at times. This ought not to be underestimated.

- Hindsight may be a wonderful thing, but open succession planning scenarios involving school governors and leadership teams make this a healthy aspect of change. Varying 'What If?' scenarios can be discussed and planned for as a result, including the inevitable moving on the Head or others.

Section 2: Sustainable Growth

5 | Tell You What, Why Don't We Ask the Pupils How They Learn Best?

It was a dull autumnal day in Hatfield, Hertfordshire, until I was treated to a ray of sunshine in the Reception Class. The teacher, Katie, oblivious to my presence, was transformed into 'Mrs Green', a visitor to the class who knew everything there was to know about gardening. As she spun that magical web of shared belief around the class, 4-year-olds showed her seedlings growing in pots made from recycled materials, whilst classmates explained how acorns and conkers helped them to count. Looking around this rich learning environment, pupil engagement was in every display, at child height, whilst the Garden Centre Shop and Outdoor Plant Stall encouraged opportunities for sorting and classifying. The environment dripped with opportunities to learn.

Our aim, after Katie's starting point, was to continue to enable these children to shape their own learning.

Many of the children at Howe Dell enter Nursery below the national values in all areas assessed. However, the progress gained due to the creative teaching and a shared love of learning between pupil and teacher is outstanding. As a School, like many with a lower than average baseline, the children achieve broadly average scores at Key Stage 1, but then, untypically, fly to exceed challenging targets set, by the time they leave Year 6. This profile is not magical; it's down to committed staff ensuring every moment matters for every child. It's exhausting, sometimes frustrating, but hugely rewarding and is only possible where those Reception children are able to be handed over to the next teacher knowing:

- They will not be perceived as 'empty vessels'.
- There is transition reporting, which includes information about the whole child, the levels of attainment, preferred learning styles, interests beyond school, people who are important to that child.
- There is respect for what has gone on before; achievements are built upon – even when Foundation Stage and Key Stage 1 curriculum design can appear to come from different universes! The children are the same people before and after that summer holiday, which is why we continue their Early Years portfolio and Foundation-styled teaching during the first term in Year 1.

Growing teams to enrich provision

In developing an environment where children learn best, we need a team of staff with a variety of approaches and skills. Katie's creativity and love of the outdoors is contagious to children in her care. Her vibrant displays, confident role play and creative ways in which she integrates child initiated learning, all encourage children to take risks, to sometimes fail, but strive for growth and development as a journey to enrich the individual.

> If you can fill the unforgiving second
> With sixty seconds worth of distance run,
> Yours is the Earth and everything that's in it
> And which is more; you'll be a man, my son!
> Rudyard Kipling, If: Brother Square Toes

Learning is a journey and after three years of a rising trend of attainment, with case studies to show excellent contextual value-added benefits, it is clear that neither an outstanding teacher, nor a collection of teachers, has anywhere near the impact of an outstanding team: my 'A Team'.

The advantage of the distributive leadership approach is that there is always someone to ask, someone who might know where to look for resources, procedures or assessment tools. No one knows all the answers – certainly no Head should set themselves up with this expectation – and the disappointment is likely to be exhausting for all concerned.

How to find out what children value

Through our Pupil Forum, children were asked 'How do you learn best?' This proved to match closely with any adult leader's perspective. Unsurprisingly, they spoke of pacey lessons with varied approaches. They valued displays to celebrate outcomes and to support them towards independence. They talked of support structures available, but also being given opportunities to try for themselves. We call this 'The Give It A Go Club', borrowed from Allstair Smith's approach, and clearly publish examples of such success each week. The outcomes, collated by Year 6, are added to all our teacher advertisements, as shown below, and their view is confidently held:

Do YOU:
Listen to children?
Play games where people can move?
Is everyone included?
Do you have listening activities as well as looking at the board activities?
Are you a teacher that doesn't mind making mistakes?
Do you use different objects, puppets and songs etc. to teach with?
Do you teach in stages – the very easy stuff to the harder stuff, because sometimes we need reminding about the easy bits?
Do you tell the children where they've gone wrong in their tests?
Do the children know their targets?
Do YOU think you can do this? All our teachers at Howe Dell can …

Key staff members were praised for thinking differently or sharing the learning journey:

'Our Deputy Head doesn't mind the children telling her that she has made a mistake. We are all in the Give It A Go Club; that means we don't mind making mistakes.'

'We like learning in different ways. Mrs Menhams uses puppets, we all sing, look at videos and talk in French to each other. Also, Mrs Menhams gets children up to have a go themselves.'

How can we enrich that learning journey for all?

By celebrating Beacon Pupils, the Give It A Go Club philosophy can be reiterated. The extract from the newsletter demonstrates the variety of reasons for achieving such an award. They celebrate those who have taken risks in learning, persevered and demonstrated strong role modelling behaviour to their peers. There are many ways to celebrate this: for us, the rosette is worn for a week, and then returned for another worthy winner. These are treasured and many a child has gone to visit family wearing this badge of honour at the weekend – or even slept with it on! An extract of the newsletter is evident below:

NEWS FROM THE CHILDREN'S COUNCIL		
This Week's Beacon Pupils are all celebrated.		
On the recommendation of the class teachers, we would like to celebrate our Beacon Pupils this week. Notes were taken by members of Year 6.		
R 1	Saiema	For really good handwriting.
R2	Ellie	Always well behaved and always working hard.
Y1 Cl1	Blessing	Doing very well in reading.
Y1 Cl2	Ellie	Really giving everything a go.
Y2	Savarah	Making a big effort in PE.
Y3	Georgina	Amazed Mrs Menhams in her swimming lesson.
Y4	Donel	Really good writing.
Y5	Ben	Starting to explain himself with confidence.
Y6	Grant	For increased maturity over the last few weeks.

Keeping all thank you letters and positive feedback in 'Happy Books' which are available in the main entrance is not only good marketing but can also show pertinent views of what children have enjoyed and found memorable and why. The why is essential, so that this strategy can be replicated:

'Year 4 were lucky to go to Green Lanes for a speed stacking competition. Ellis and Callum were 2 children out of 30 schools to get to the final. We represented Welwyn and Hatfield. Four other boys and girls also came. Unfortunately, we didn't win it but were happy to have made it so far.'

Quote from KS2 report.

Themed weeks are very popular, including dress up days and special visitors. But what evaluations say the children value most is the carousel. This is an afternoon of mixed-age workshops led by staff; the children attempt four sessions in an afternoon. They need to be skills-based and linked to the theme of the week. An example of what is on offer is evident in our Beacon Challenge Week, where children were introduced to trying something for the first time.

When asked via Pupil Forum when learning is most exciting, the children explained it was when Drama was used in Science, or Music was used in Maths, as this challenged their way of thinking. This happens in many schools, but perhaps giving children a greater choice in demonstrating learning using different learning styles might impact further on attainment? It certainly motivates in an inclusive way.

Can pupils work alongside adults as equals on a shared agenda?

♦ By organizing a Learning Walk with children and/or governors, a greater awareness of the child's perceptions comes into play. For example, children could say that art skills were being used for observational flower drawings, to support a Science lesson, but as all had water colours and the same type of flowers, this was not seen as creative. However, for the learning objective 'To look closely and begin to label parts of a daffodil' it was a motivational way of getting young children to look carefully and look longer. This was a study evaluated by children as young as 7.

♦ What was interesting from the pupil's involved in the learning walk was their clear understanding that creativity was possible across all subjects, not just the arts:
'In science, dance helps to show the movements in solids, liquids and gases to show you how particles move.' Pupil Forum, 2010

♦ By giving children technology to record their findings, from digital cameras to inexpensive child-friendly DVD recorders, a different perspective is obtained of a route walked daily. The angle of images and what is noticed by a small child will be different from that seen by a tall adult!

♦ Moreover, when given a break over lunchtime, they ran in and seized the cameras. 'Creative learning's happening all over the place," said Adam, aged 7, 'and we're missing it!' The children were able to photograph learning happening in clubs run by staff, a dance club completely organized by Year 6 which had a blind child fully engaged with her peers, as well as free play at lunchtimes. Later that term, an idea appeared in the suggestion box, sharing the lasting impact of the Learning Walk with a wider group of children.

♦ Once outcomes are shared, the ripple effect is apparent, as others justify their suggestions in the light of recent learning walk foci:

♦ 'Can we run a club for Key Stage 1 called FUN KIDS, to include drama, quizzes, dancing, art and athletics to help with their health and creativity? We hope this has convinced you we are doing lunchtime learning!' (Megan and Lauren)

Starting out – what do you ask and how?

In doing any self-evaluation work with pupils, there needs to be consideration of:

◆ Age and stage of the participants.
◆ Time needed to plan and present the questions.
◆ How these will be reported back and to whom.

There are a number of tools on the School website, which range from the registration activity 'Hands Up Survey' to quotations in response to Wonder Days. A question such as 'How does it feel to walk into the classroom if you are late in the morning?' has since been shared with parents and published in our prospectus, as available via the School website. An extract below shows the power of the pupil voice in this context.

> If I am late I don't like going into class because everyone already knows what they are doing.
> 'It makes my tummy feel funny when I am late because I might be missing something important …
> Using a questionnaire from Ofsted's website for Key Stage 2 was useful for checking that we knew what we thought we knew, but it also uncovered an issue about a previous Year 6 group in the summer term and how intimidating their behaviour appeared to some Year 5 pupils. This was followed up via an assembly on personal safety with an anti-bullying theme and puppets. Such strategies are invaluable in explaining difficult issues, but encouraging to have the children to play the role of expert advisers. Staff get their script prior to the event, so that they can follow this up thoroughly – a really successful strategy. A possible script is available via the companion website.

A Time of change? Include your clients!

When leadership changes in school, there is an ideal time to talk to children, but to also get governors to do so, too. In a governor-led discussion, alongside lots of positives, there was a feeling that not enough drama happened in lessons and assemblies. As a result, Drama as a Vehicle for Learning training was offered to new teachers, teaching assistants and some midday supervisors, so that story boxes, playmaking and role play areas became evident through Key Stage 1 and were trialled in Year 4. Not only do the children love it, but so too do staff!

How is the impact measurable?

Some evaluations give data-led statistics, to give a flavour of pupils' views. Some of these can be collated by pupils themselves, as already demonstrated via our Pupil Forum feedback. More evaluation tools are available in Chapter 6 and on the companion website.

The most lasting impact may not 'fit into boxes' quite so easily. Hence the value of case studies is seen. On an annual basis, encourage each teacher to give a case study for each core subject, to demonstrate the impact of personalized learning for a child. These are powerful documents indeed and tell a variety of stories from:

◆ The Year 4 boy who was a reluctant writer but keen to introduce ducks to our wetland area and did so via ongoing written communication with key adults. His writing moved on, and the ducks arrived!

◆ The Traveller child, often absent, whose reading moved on two and a half years in a year due to excellent relationship building and at times 'tough love' with Mum from a committed class teacher.

◆ The Year 6 girl with low self-esteem who grew to love Maths through the support of a one–to-one tutor. 'You are my mode, never the mean and above the median' she wrote in her thank you card: she exceeded her targets in end of year tests.

If we get it right in primary education, children's lasting impressions are not tests or grazed knees on a cold November playground. Long-term memories should be steeped in pirate and princesses parties, growing and harvesting their own produce, with Mrs Chalmers, Wonder Days, family learning and a chance to shape their learning to make it their own.

Katie as 'Mrs Green' is one of many teachers in role across the country making a world full of questions and puzzles accessible to more of our children. But what's next for these children? How will secondary schools continue to build upon who they are and fulfil their potential through what they will become? When asked about learning in five years time and what they would prefer, our children gave this response:

How we would like to learn?	No. of votes
Outdoors	27
Bigger classes	10
Smaller classes	15
At home	12
Through links with the community	16

Other ideas were:
- Learn with a different year group.
- Brain training on DSI.
- Chance to grow crops and have chickens.

All of these suggestions are now embedded in what we do: the spirit of 'Mrs Green' lives on!

Key points for consideration

- Ensure transition from one academic year is given quality time and is inclusive of the whole child. Allocating a training day to this is time well spent.
- Use Pupil Forum, pupil representation in discussion groups, interview days and visits from governors, so that they have varied opportunities to tell you how they learn best. Many examples of these are available via the School website.
- If introducing Learning Walks, ensure all staff are well briefed and that these are led by a member of the leadership team. This is not a chance for children to assess teachers. Creating the right climate is essential. Moreover, update performance management and monitoring policies to ensure these are understood to be short and informed classroom discussions.
- Always remember, the children are your clients. Therefore asking them quickly and in greater depth what they value and what is the next step for your school are essential means to school improvement.

♦ Follow up difficult scenarios via assemblies using puppets to distance the issue from a child who may have bought it to your attention – but warn your staff if they are due to play an active role! Some examples of when scenarios would benefit from this approach are available through the companion website.

♦ Finally, seek questions you or the children really want to know the answer to, whether it is to do with ethos or curriculum, and test out perceptions using a variety of strategies, to reinforce the accuracy of the findings.

6 | Assessing Areas of Weakness: Self-Evaluation Tools

It was the first morning of a School journey to the Essex coast. Ellie was walking with me to the Lighthouse Ship where we stay.

'Mrs Massey, on a School journey, you seem shorter,' she remarked. 'Probably due to me wearing trainers not heels,' I replied.

'And your eyes look smaller ...' she added.

'No time for make-up here,' I joked.

'You are different in other ways, too,' she continued.

'Really? In what way?' I asked.

'Well, at School, in the mornings, you are always smiling. Here you seem quite grumpy!' she explained.

What I **wanted** to retort was that this was probably due to the fact that the last child settled at midnight last night, the first one woke at 5 a.m.!

Asking questions about what you **think** you know isn't always a comfortable process, but it reaffirms, challenges and can move practice from good to outstanding.

Self-evaluation is a process which ought to have a health warning such as 'There be dragons', as one might find things that are not welcome: a time-consuming questionnaire doesn't necessarily produce useful information. The School self-evaluation audit on the companion website might be a good place to start! Many other tools can be seen in operation via our School website.

Pupil voice: the first port of call for the truth

The walk with Ellie was one of many conversations we all have with children in our schools. What is memorable was how she was evaluating what she *thought* she knew, whilst making sense of new information gained. How can we best tap this resource to:

◆ evaluate and modify teaching and learning?
◆ consider how best to spend additional money?
◆ modify the very ethos of our organizations?

Questionnaires are an ideal starting point for a quick review of a specific area for development, from reviewing likes and dislikes on the school dinner menu to evaluating key events. However, this is not the full story: information collated needs to be quantitative (with statistics) but also *qualitative*. For example, when offering the School cook the outcomes of the meals survey, showing children didn't like broccoli, she said, 'I could have told you that, by seeing what children choose, hearing what they say – and noticing how much is thrown away.'

When children lead the questions and data collation, it becomes more powerful and when reported on a lively choice of colour and content powerpoint slides by four 10-year-olds, the data is owned, as evident in the following slide. A full rainbow-coloured version is available on the companion website.

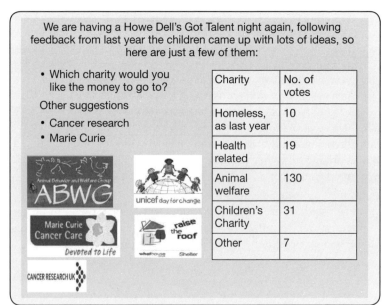

However, quotations to reinforce the views held, give a greater depth to what is thought. Hence the value of teachers as scribes becomes important, or use of recording devices during the debates. Otherwise, the *context* of the quotations (e.g. to which question the response was made and sometimes the age and stage of the respondent) may be lost.

A worked example with Year 2 and above

In creating questionnaires for children, add a place for additional comments, as well as a voting option. Teachers will value this dual structure, incorporating a hands up survey, speedily completed at registration. The PowerPoint on the companion website reviews the Wonder Day provided by a wildlife photographer, with quantitative data as follows:

My favourite pictures were of: *Tigers*	*Birds*	*Deer*	*Monkeys*	*Other*
114	3	2	27	0

The place I learned most about was:	*India*	*London*	*England*	*Other*
	89	29	16	0

I thought our Wonder Day was:	*Excellent*	*Good*	*OK*	*Not interesting*
	108	30	0	0

The pupil views, to add some qualitative input, could later be collated from a class-based circle time, or planned as a class assembly, with a final section for staff comment, aiming to summarize outcomes. What are the benefits? Well, it's all on one piece of paper, but tackles three tasks. These quotations strongly reinforce the power of quantitative data, showing a high level of engagement far beyond the initial figures arising from the hands up survey. The level of pupil reflection evident in this qualitative data is deeper and impacted upon how Wonder Days were planned following this success:

- ◆ 'Lovely writing from the day.' Y2
- ◆ 'I enjoyed writing the letters to tell people not to kill animals.' Y3
- ◆ 'I didn't know there were so many tigers in India.' Y3
- ◆ 'The pictures were great and we learnt a lot.' Y4
- ◆ 'I learnt more about wildlife.' Y4

- 'It would have been good to see and learn more about how the camera works.' Y4
- 'I really enjoyed the Wonder Day because I learned that skills like perseverance, determination and patience are needed in photography, but also in my school work.' Y5
- 'I enjoyed the tips on taking photos.' Y6
- 'It made us realize that there is wildlife all around.' Y6

Scaffold the skills

When extending children's writing skills, there is a general agreement that modelling *how* to write in terms of structure and content is important. It is the same with self-evaluation.

- The tools on the website for Pupil Forum are starting points; initially adult-led coaching will be necessary in collating the results. However, this lessens in time, especially if the children are shown that the outcomes shape future provision, thus having real purpose.
- Likewise, by using assembly or curriculum time with a story-based theme, it is possible to initiate very young children to the notion of listening to views and the power of voting. This was introduced at one school by using the story of *Old Bear*, by Jane Hissey, where this tired old toy is relegated to the loft. Rather than start at the beginning of the well known story, the centrefold was introduced, asking why he was not with the other toys. Then by using small toys (from a certain burger company based on characters from Pooh Bear) the children were asked to determine who would be the best at rescuing Old Bear.
- 'Tigger, because he can bounce and bounce and wouldn't give up.'
- 'Pooh, because he could make a tower of honey pots – and he's a bear, so they already have something in common.'

The solutions are endless, but no answer is wrong. During the week, Children's Council representatives took to the playground and canvassed their peers on behalf of the Pooh Bear characters. Once the results were announced, the cheers were heartfelt and a lesson in empowerment was learnt. Furthermore, the impact of voting and contributing a view had been demonstrated.

Tracking what you already do

Less obvious ways of evaluating provision with children can include keeping a log of children who are sent to the Head for Children's Hour or on an ad hoc basis to share their work. Our analysis raised questions about why these children were singled out for praise and for what subjects. It gave us a chance to review processes to guard against gender stereotypes (boys for Maths, girls for Literacy, for example). The data and analysis to inform school improvement is available via the companion website.

The Suggestion Box has already been mentioned at length in Chapter 5, but a response that doesn't just say *what* has been raised as ideas for development and whether this has been successful, *but uses it as a start for a new term's assembly, reaffirms the power of those who 'get involved'*. The extract below demonstrates this.

Suggestion	Response
I think Jackie Morris, the author and illustrator, should come back and visit us again, but this time instead of one day, come for at least two days so It's worth the drive! **Bow**	Jackie is booked again for a visit in March 2011 and plans to do an exhibition of her beautiful paintings here. She is also keen to email you about the publication of *Panda's Child* which will be published in 2013. (She read this to you as its very first audience).
Can we please have a Children's Quiz Night? **Luke**	Good idea. Maybe when you are on the Children's Council you could organize this? I am sure the PSA would help?

Self-evaluation can combat niggles head-on

If 'playground drums' are telling you there is an issue which is causing some grumbles, but it has yet to become a key concern, self-evaluation is the way forward. Adapting the Ofsted parent questionnaire to include a comments section with a tear-off slip, encouraging those who wish to join a parent council, is a good place to start. It is fully inclusive and gives an avenue for a self-elected group to bridge the gap between playground and perhaps the formality of the role of parent governor. An example of how this was used at Howe Dell is available via the companion website.

As a result of our 'mock Ofsted questionnaire', we now have 13 parents on a parent voice group (self-named); they replied alongside the School to any issues arising from the questionnaire. They have also:

♦ elected class representatives amongst their number;
♦ contributed to Quality Mark and Investors In People preparation;
♦ initiated e-safety reviews to be more parent friendly;
♦ considered the leasing arrangements of bikes to older pupils;
♦ submitted photograph and introductory paragraph, which has been collated into a PowerPoint to raise their profile with other parents.

This approach has been highly effective in time management too: all items listed were achieved in the space of two meetings in a term, plus immediate input into future plans and school development on a broader agenda was gained.

One member explained how she gets quite angry if a parent is negative about the school, especially if they don't go through the channels available, such as reading the newsletter, meeting with staff or completing a questionnaire. It was a very impassioned view and she was not alone!' By including parent voice feedback on the published report of questionnaire outcomes, alongside the Head's response, gave a peer-led perspective which was very powerful. Likewise, take a specific issue such as 'voluntary contributions' to parents via a questionnaire. By explaining that choices do need to be made about cost and provision and asking them to log what they value most, quantitative as well as qualitative processes can again be included.

Comments and Quotes for Parents	School Response
'I think it would be a good idea to name and shame non-payers.'	Whist sympathetic to this view, we would not ever want to put children and families on low income in this situation.
'I do not wish to pay more or subsidize those who don't pay so their child can go.'	No one pays a cost to subsidize anyone else's child. Legally, parents are asked to pay a 'voluntary contribution' towards their own child's tuition.

Becoming increasingly frustrated with a poor response to swimming donations, without which lessons were not viable, the questionnaire was created. Backing up the questionnaire, follow-up texts and individual phone calls have been time consuming but necessary in order to get a good level of response.

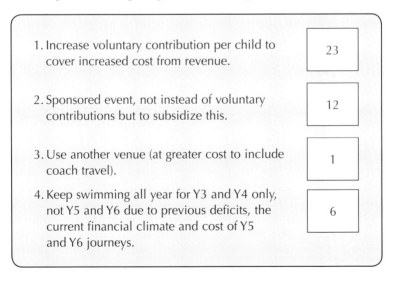

1. Increase voluntary contribution per child to cover increased cost from revenue.	23
2. Sponsored event, not instead of voluntary contributions but to subsidize this.	12
3. Use another venue (at greater cost to include coach travel).	1
4. Keep swimming all year for Y3 and Y4 only, not Y5 and Y6 due to previous deficits, the current financial climate and cost of Y5 and Y6 journeys.	6

As seen, however many sensible suggestions you receive, you still cannot prepare yourself for the exasperation from the lone voice who wants swimming to be *more expensive and further away*: no one ever said leadership was straightforward! In the long run, swimming non payment is all but eradicated at Howe Dell, perhaps an example of how leaders in School need to remember to 'pick your battles' to ensure commitment of time and energy can be applied effectively!

Getting our After School Club trained to collate parent views on palm-held devices resulted in useful evaluative data. Parents said they were more comfortable talking to children than either filling in forms or answering questions directly to a member of staff – as they didn't want to appear rude. The company Adroit was engaged with the School via our extended Schools consortium, but still at a considerable cost to the schools involved. However, as a tool it was useful to review against other information. See www.adroitconsulting.com.

How to get staff involved

The same rules apply as with previous groups: start small and specific and grow from there. An experienced leader will be comfortable with having a range of questions on large pieces of paper, encouraging colleagues to write anything that comes to mind on post-its beneath the headings that appeal. But this is not always very useful as an early approach, as 'there be dragons', notably:

- Certain colleagues (who may still be unknown to the new leader) can sabotage by dominating proceedings, producing 'death by post-it'.
- The leader then feels a need to achieve the suggestions on the post-its in a far too broad focus to actually have any long-term impact.
- Therefore, questionnaires with an Ofsted grading 1 to 4 (outstanding to poor) is easily transferable to Ofsted-based evidence, a comments box and future development giving scope to those who may wish to step forward: these may well be future project leaders. A pro forma for training/evaluation is available via the companion website. (Sometimes, with an inherited and perhaps divided team, ensuring a high profile and specific brief for someone who may challenge rather than support, can lead to the development of a good professional relationship, where there might otherwise have been confrontation.)
- Seeking views, and acting upon these, develops ownership and opportunity. We have introduced a pro forma for all staff training which has improved organization and relevance to staff

development. Encouraging staff to consider how this will impact on their role also ensures commitment and ownership in their own professional growth (available via website).

In my fifth year of leading Howe Dell, I feel confident in opening the floor of self-evaluation to our 78 colleagues across the School, Children's Centre, Day Care and extended services. Nevertheless, when planning whole site training my aims are always to have:

◆ themes for which no one is a total expert;
◆ themes which are inclusive of everyone;
◆ opportunities to laugh!
◆ a purpose which is real and relevant to moving the organization forward;
◆ chances to talk, dance, move, draw;
◆ a revisitation of the vision and how it continually adapts as we evolve.

One useful shared focus is the Every Child Matters agenda with the five outcomes for every child:

◆ Being Healthy.
◆ Being Safe.
◆ Making a positive contribution.
◆ Emotional health.
◆ Economic wellbeing.

As a result of this, in our bid to move from a good to outstanding provider, teams mixing all departments of the organization were divided to review good and outstanding grading from Ofsted criteria. It was staggering how perceptive all groups were: the outcomes from whole staff matched those on the School self-evaluation documentation, updated by me over the holidays. Comments such as the following prove a point: 'Our safeguarding procedures are outstanding, but so much is new, we need it embedded to move to that grade, so suggest that this is graded good at present' (Kelly, Day Care worker).

Likewise, asking staff under the five outcomes to 'Bring A Story to Life' unveiled case studies of excellent practice, which celebrated the untold stories, not sentimentally, and then drawn up into a document, logging the intervention used and the impact as a result. A worked sample is demonstrated here, and a pro forma is available on the companion website.

Being Healthy – Children bringing in unhealthy food at lunchtimes (fizzy drinks, crisps, etc.).	Alerted parents and made a rule of only water/healthy foods at lunchtimes. MSA Awards introduced and stickers celebrating those with healthy lunch boxes.	Healthier diets for children and 'consistency' throughout school.
Being Healthy – Child wouldn't eat or drink anything at nursery.	Sticker charts. Communication with parents. Encouragement and one-to-one.	The child now eats and drinks healthily at nursery.
Being Healthy – Child refused to eat any fruit or vegetables.	Staff encouraged her to try a tiny taste each day. Growing fruit & vegetables on site has developed interest and confidence in trying new foods.	When she came to lunchtimes she would try everything – including fruit and vegetables.
Being Healthy and Emotional Wellbeing – Cost of taking children out and family time (pressure).	Children's Centre organized swimming activities and drumming for the community.	Wellbeing/health. Over 50 attended. Future events planned.

Building an evaluative community

Rome wasn't built in a day – nor was our new community in Hatfield! However, tackling issues such as parking and congestion hasn't resolved all concerns, but by being brave enough to host an open meeting with press invited, action plans were formed and new partnerships began. Since then, a local councillor, who came to a Visitors' Day held on the last Friday of every month, is now a governor and we forge forward with parking, extended use of whole site and an environmental project: it's a start.

Self-evaluation does not always have to focus on the problems; sometimes it's good to develop a shared project from demonstrating what a local community is proud of. Inspired by prayer flags at the Eden Project, the shared enthusiasm of two parents with creative and technical expertise and the World Cup theme tune 'Wave Your Flag' by Knaan, we have engaged over 500 participants in drawing collectively or individually, through open invitation and planned events, what they would want to celebrate about our organization.

Self-evaluation can be multi-sensory. A group of staff depicted us growing children's minds and setting our pledge to reach for the stars, to touch the trees. This has been used against the review of our vision and aims in developing our new curriculum.

Self-evaluation really is at best with the philosophy that to be lifelong learners we need to constantly review and develop in order to shape understanding for the next generation.

Key points for consideration

♦ Many outlines are available for use or adaption via the website.
♦ Consider the timing of self-evaluative tasks – the questionnaire or the event is the easy bit; collating and implementing outcomes takes longer.
♦ Ensure there is sufficient time in the planning process to ensure

sustainability for administration colleagues to whom some collation can be delegated.

◆ How and where to publish outcomes is also key: the aim should not be to alienate those who have contributed, but show their view has been valued but put into context alongside those views of the majority. To belittle or ignore a view can exacerbate frustrations and undermine the role of the individual in this process. At times, a whole School event or formal presentation, or perhaps a change in procedure, is more appropriate than summarizing in a newsletter.

◆ Give teachers sufficient warning if a project or task is imminent, with clarity about time required and deadlines. (Is it a registration task – or a lesson? If the latter, give at least two weeks' notice, ideally half a term.)

◆ Use the Ofsted website – there's some good resources and isn't it better to know where those dragons are? Ideally not so close to an anticipated inspection that it becomes overkill: death by too many questionnaires is unpleasant for the recipient, but also frustrating for the sender, as response will be diluted and less useful.

◆ For children, use stories as a means to model evaluative techniques within lessons or assemblies.

◆ Suggestion Boxes are invaluable, but need responding to regularly.

◆ 'Visitors' Days' are a good source of data for community cohesion – who comes into School and why they do so is useful to collate annually.

◆ Don't forget complaints! 'Happy Books' can be filled with thank you messages and shared with as wide a community as possible. Complaints logged and reported (anonymised) to a Full Governing Body help put them into context: 'We have 12 complaints this year across the School, Children's Centre, Day Care and extended services. Five are from the same parent, who has now left!'

◆ Remember that when working with very young children, timing is key. There is little point, for example, doing a hands up survey on 'How I travelled To School' after lunch … no one will remember! To make this useful, accurate and practical for the teacher, notice needs to be given: electronic copies sent beforehand and paper copies in the morning registers both act as prompts.

7 | Meet Them at the Gates: Engaging with Parents, Governors and the Wider Community

In our first half term at the Runway, Year 6 pupils did their usual collection of Harvest Festival produce, alongside so many primary schools across the UK. Following a whole School assembly, led by a local vicar, with parents attending, the children knocked on doors to distribute these harvest gifts.

As well as the thank you letters which followed, the most powerful outcome was from an elderly lady called Christine who said, 'I know the School's for the children, but what will it do for the likes of me?'

One pupil asked 'Well, what do you want it to do?'

The first step towards community cohesion had been taken.

In fact, it transpired that Christine and two of her friends (one who owned a laptop, but had never switched it on) wanted a chance to develop their ICT skills. This was relatively easy to sort, by using an hour of our ICT technician's time and risk assessing elderly and often physically frail visitors to site. This became an example of a truly symbiotic relationship, as Christine and her friends spread the word of what they were doing within School, even speaking on behalf of Howe Dell at Residents' Association meetings. More importantly, Christine became a regular visitor to many events we hosted. She told me at a Christmas service that she kept a special file of Howe Dell events, sharing this with her grandchild. It successfully bridged the generation gap with a shared agenda: 'Look what I did at MY school today!'

Don't underestimate individuals in building the bigger picture

Ofsted is very clear that outstanding provision in community cohesion needs to have evidence of local neighbourhood links, regional contacts and then global awareness. However, this is only achievable and real if we build cohesion starting with individual relationships.

Sometimes, the very title of 'Headteacher' can be an obstacle in reaching out to community groups, based upon their own childhood experience. However, a school surrounded by a building site is not devoid of skills and attributes; moreover, when an influx of new people arrive on an estate they often share one issue: isolation. Indeed, our links with the Polish community began on our first day, when a Polish plasterer on site was able to communicate with a new child in Year 6, as well as completing the builders' finish in a number of classrooms!

Where do you start?

♦ By being on the playground daily before and after school, a Head can begin to recognize parents, feedback gems of information about individual children and reinforce that their child has been noticed *positively*. It also stops small worries turning into larger issues, as questions can be answered as they arise, and gives early warning of community issues or disputes too! The playground is a wonderful source of often fascinating intrigue!

♦ Likewise, a pupil knocking on doors accompanied by staff, to notify residents of school events, perhaps to apologize in advance for any congestion or even to give them a personal invitation to attend, really pays dividends. (We had thank you notes following this approach which warned that the road may be closed when the wind turbine was delivered: a little forethought avoided possible police engagement and public disorder!)

♦ Try informal coffee mornings, not just for parents but also for representatives of local businesses, followed by a tour of the school led by children, to reinforce the school values: the pupils are the best ambassadors.

♦ Class groups, playing in the local park, can bring the face of the school beyond the school gates with what has only ever achieved a positive outcome.

- Over time (and Rome wasn't built in a day!) having informal governor presence near refreshments available for school events, including parent–teacher consultation appointments, encourages the philosophy of openness and the school's willingness to listen to its stakeholders.
- Set up a monthly assembly which is not just open to parents but publicized as a 'Visitors' Day' and log the different reasons for their visit. An annual collation of this information gives rich pickings for community cohesion evidence, when logging the variation of visitor purpose.
- Before business representatives leave, refer them to a contact in the school, which could equally be a subject leader, as a means of spreading the workload and extending partnerships beyond the Head.
- Check out local notice boards to see what other groups meet in the area, or ask your Children's Council to do this for you. Many an assembly slot can be filled by volunteers displaying skills ranging from karate to puppy walking for the blind.
- Have a family and friends section on your website, which reaffirms the community relationships your organization values. *Be careful to agree with governors what boundaries to this publicity you are prepared to be associated with: a school encouraging healthy eating may think twice about sponsorship from an international burger retailer!*
- If not a new estate, perhaps developing the reputation of your school might be through delivery of handcrafted Christmas cards or gifts, to show elderly neighbours in particular, the positive side of young people in your community. (We did an apple bake with a local secondary school to use their facilities and to also include teenagers in the project. It also successfully marketed a positive image of *youth*, rather than just rebranding one school.)
- Use technology to highlight key stakeholders. Following a parent questionnaire which suggested not all governors or their roles were known, a weekly profile was added to newsletters. This was followed up by a photograph and introductory statement on a PowerPoint via the School website, including each member of the board. This method can be used for other groups, such as community links, friends of the school or parent groups.

Key individuals in every community

Religious leaders are invaluable to schools in developing community cohesion. A Methodist minister, new and committed to the area, knocked on the door one day in early December, introduced herself and asked if she could help in any way.

I immediately signed her up to our Advent-themed 'Positive Beginnings' sessions. These are for parents or carers with children under the age of 5, sometimes but not always attending due to a referral from another professional agency. The sessions model behaviour strategies and consistency of care, and provide learning through play opportunities for adult and child.

'Reverend Nina', as she was soon referred to, joined in the Advent activities, chatted to parents and carers and let them know what was available over the Christmas holiday. She became part of what I jokingly called my 'Christmas package', but it was more than that: she offered home visits and friendship to many who were new and often lonely, on what was still a partially built housing estate. It wasn't just about adopting a local minister. Reverend Nina rode a motorbike, arrived at assemblies in helmet and leathers, beneath which was her dog collar: she had immediate impact! She was a warm, positive person, an intelligent critical friend and a great listener for me and anyone within and beyond Howe Dell. By January 2008, she was a School Governor, soon to be Vice Chair of Governors and chair of our Children's Centre steering group. Nina's approachability has been reinforced by School assemblies, visits to the classrooms with the RE subject leader, and has since run staff training on RE development. Most recently, she has enabled Methodist-led youth work to grow in the area, often using our site to facilitate this, whilst her Saturday Morning Club, at the adjacent and previously underused community hall, is teeming with families, embarking on art and craft as well as forging new friendships.

Contacts with other religious groups also include a satellite link, enabling the hosting of Polish church services, whilst Muslim and Hindu weddings have also taken place in our building. Some of these have created income for the School, but also reaffirm our inclusion of all.

Food, music and dance can bring a community together. From Hare Krishna representatives providing food for all, to a Rabbi teaching children how to make candles, everything is possible. But it does need time to develop the mutual respect and understanding of some shared aims. Clarity of purpose is essential to enable success, rather than the outcome exacerbating the situation! More easily attainable projects could include:

- Community picnics or 'Bring a Plate', using the School site (ensuring that ingredients are listed if potentially sensitive to certain groups).
- A Community Fete, hosted by the School, but encouraging stalls from local groups, who keep the profit of their stalls. To reach out beyond the School gate, half the proceeds from such an event at Howe Dell paid for a community notice board in the local park, an emblem of shared information and bridge building.
- Celebrate such projects through the local press! A good news story of benefit to more than one group sells papers!
- Link the School website to local groups, such as Residents' Associations or Neighbourhood Watch, to enable shared agendas to be evident but also to reinforce that these links are valued by the School.

Growing governor competency

Nina is one of a group of very strong governors we have at Howe Dell and there lies another pathway to community cohesion. We are now fortunate, due to our reputation locally and the ecological features of the site, to recruit governors easily, but that has not always been the case. Some practical tips to aid consistency and to get the best from your governors might include:

- It is crucial to build on key strengths, rather than overwhelm these wonderful volunteers with responsibility for everything. Failure will follow if, armed with only a veneer of knowledge, they are expected to tackle a huge agenda. This can be completed through a skills' audit, available via the companion website, Chapter 2.
- An individual meeting with the Head to establish mutual expectations is also important, especially when governors are visiting on a more formal basis, such as paired lesson observations or learning walks, from which a report will be shared with staff and governors. Sometimes, the trickiest to manage can be governors who have had experience of working in education. Their knowledge base may be invaluable, but how this is applied to *your* organization needs clarity of what the role is – and sometimes,

what it is not. Written notes copied for Head or subject leader give immediate feedback to staff; these notes ought to be checked by the Head prior to distribution for drafting into a formal report. A prescribed outline for all to follow aids consistency. Examples of a master for governor visits, schedules to apply, completed reports from old site and new, for both subjects and themes, and an outlines for reports, are all available via the companion website.

◆ Concerns of a sensitive nature, such as behaviour in a particular class, can be noted on the back of the form to be discussed confidentially with the Head on the day of the visit. This enables the Head to follow up as appropriate, but still values the role of 'critical friend'.

◆ Governors often bring professional links (supermarkets, banks, national or small companies), which are perfect opportunities for community cohesion.

◆ Many larger organizations have funding and volunteers available to support local projects. By successfully encouraging governors to invite groups from their workplace to visit school, have a tour

Brian Dummer, no longer Chair of Governors but still active as link governor for History, Chair of the Curriculum Committee co-ordinating cycling proficiency … and dancing at the pace of exuberant 6-year-olds!

led by the children and attend a sharing assembly, outcomes have included:

✓ Developed links with the university for teaching and learning.

✓ Extended expertise and support for ICT, including our new radio station.

✓ Volunteers from organizations to create allotments.

◆ Retired governors have time and interests to utilize, and can often engage the extended community in many ways. One such example is Brian, an ex-Head who has led country dancing, cycling proficiency and is a regular visitor to School. His energy is boundless; he was chair of governors and provides insight and leadership to curriculum development.

His hobbies and interests are extensive and include creating opportunities for local schools to sing together at a Hatfield church in an event entitled 'Songs of Praise'. He is also an 'artefact' for World War Two, and visits Year 4 to become part of their research on this topic. His completed governor visit report is available on the companion website, to show the depth of impact possible from engaging such resourceful individuals.

Getting out and about!

Contacts with local businesses can begin with Reception children being taught to cross the road, with support of a local police officer, or older children helping to pack shopping at a supermarket. However, as with Reverend Nina, lasting relationships are initiated by personal contact. One example of how this has impacted upon learning has been through our Year 5 engagement with the water board, Veolia. Beginning with visits to and from both organizations, there have been voluntary groups in the freezing January weather conditions erecting fencing for our allotments. The fencing was heavily built and a large financial investment as it is made from recycled plastic bags and therefore had a strong ethical message.

The Year 5 children visited Veolia, saw and reported on their eco credentials, set targets and returned to evaluate whether these had been reached. They also set up a display over lunchtime at Veolia and talked to employees about sustainable development. Our Deputy Head talked with delight about observing Rebecca, aged 10, walking towards a Veolia member of staff and asking, 'Would you like me to explain what biodiversity is?'

The relationship continues, as does the chance to improve provision for both organizations. Gifts such as water butts provided by Veolia have impacted on reception children and above, now independently watering their garden and crops.

When it doesn't quite go to plan, patience and a sense of humour are vital!

Day-to-day dealings with the community can result in stronger cohesion, but not all projects are an instant success. Like many schools, parking and traffic congestion is a daily irritation at Howe Dell and at times due to the unadopted roads there have been incidents of road rage. The joy rider losing control of his car in the middle of the night, crashing through our fence and landing on the climbing frame, remains the most memorable!

Following attempts to resolve this community issue from *inside* Howe Dell by having facilities staff on duty in an attempt to alleviate parking, it was clear that we were not lawful in trying to resolve traffic management *outside* the School gates. But no one seemed clear about who *was* responsible. Hence a working party met, representing the Town Council, County Council, developer, Police, Residents' Association and School, resulting in dropped curbs, temporary speed restrictions and bus stops being planned. However, this did not mean the end of the story! Once communication faltered, a clamping company was directed to erect signage and clamp parents not parking within a minimal area outside the School. This was unworkable, as despite acquiring free bus transport for 80 children from the old site, there was insufficient parking for parents dropping and going on to work. We provided facilities staff and a Children's Centre outreach worker for the car park to ensure children arrived safely from 8.30 a.m., but when I was away in Brazil judging for Microsoft, the School Leadership Team had to contend with angry parents, some of whom had returned with axle grinders to release their cars and, yes, the inevitable front page spread.

Take brave risks, but give yourself planning time to orchestrate these; the outcome may not be what you planned, but can still have benefits previously unforeseen

On my return, we talked about where this had gone wrong. Predominantly, it was clear that the timing of changes to parking procedures had been catastrophic. A classic example of 'he who shouts loudest' appeared to dictate the way forward for this community problem. I tried to resolve this but hit endless brick walls. As a result, I decided to write to all relevant parties and invite them to an open meeting, hosted at Howe Dell. The aim was to:

♦ celebrate outcomes from previous successful collaboration on this issue;
♦ demonstrate the lengths Howe Dell had gone to in order to resolve this issue;
♦ give stakeholders a chance to share views in mixed groups;
♦ build a way forward with a shared agenda.

It was a huge risk. Would people come? Would it turn into an angry, aggressive event, of which I would publicly lose control? I thought very hard about all these issues and others and as a result, and in order to create a positive atmosphere:

♦ Welcomed children *with* their parents/carers (also reinforcing that pupil voice matters, even when adults are finding resolution a challenge). My hope that the children's presence would curb aggression was successful.
♦ Personally phoned and wrote to organizations, attempting to forge a direct link with named individuals where possible.
♦ Agreed to press coverage, again a risk, but felt at least that way a reporter would see views at first hand.
♦ I also led and chaired the meeting, beginning with a PowerPoint to show how all possible successes to date were recognized, but to gain an undisputed leadership role in the proceedings.

Preparation for this process was huge, but necessary. There were notes taken and circulated to all who attended. Some of the more hostile early contributions were redirected to organizations responsible for the roads, who did not attend. A further questionnaire for pupils, parents, Day Care and Children's Centre users was collated, outcomes published via the De Havilland Residents' Association, including suggestions such as:

- Voluntary one way system.
- Extension of parking area.

Parents were invited to write to me with evidence of clamping on that first day of introduction and I was encouraged to apply to Community Chest funding for reimbursement as a goodwill gesture. Whilst a Polish parent, who could not read the new signage, was reimbursed, the other bids were unsuccessful. Therefore I used some Head's consultancy money for a token donation to those parents, again as an act of goodwill. This was logged as a one-off gesture and would not be viable to be repeated. However, in terms of public relations it showed us to be an organization doing our utmost to help what was a community and not just a School issue.

Since then, we have reapplied, with the support of a local councillor, and successfully acquired a £2,500 Community Chest grant to buy 15 cycles, helmets and locks to introduce a lease project encouraging children to cycle to School. This project was presented back to the community as children demonstrated cycling proficiency skills in the arena at the School Fete.

A further councillor has since joined our Governing Body and aims to work with one of our teachers on gaining funding to support wildlife in the School grounds. She has recently taken up the parking mantle again, and so it begins once more!

Not all community cohesion has to be challenging: it can be a natural extension to what is already going on in School. One example is a themed week which was encouraging the celebration of diversity in our community. During the week, artists, storytellers and dancers came to work with the children – photographs and work arising from this event oozed from every classroom. Children's Centre and Day Care also contributed via our Dress up Day, which focused on a costume and fact file celebrating a food, a hero or monument from a known place in the world.

On the final evening, we opened the site to the local community for an International evening, asking people to come and set up a stall celebrating their culture. We had 200 visitors at a time when this estate was still embryonic, food from Afghanistan to Turkey, African drumming, henna hand painting, Indian dancing and an impromptu fashion show for children who had returned to School in their costumes. It was a perfect opportunity to talk to people who were new

Dressing up ranged from Van Gogh with a bandaged ear, London Bridge, to the Statue of Liberty, with pizza thrown in for good measure!

to Hatfield and who have since read stories, given workshops for our children, even enriching our knowledge of our Hatfield community.

There are many opportunities that can enrich community cohesion via celebratory, big events. Perhaps the contrast to that is the Remembrance Assembly we hosted where there was a table to recognize family members associated with wars today and in the past, local residents came and represented all the armed services, the School entrance and assembly had a sentry of three army cadets, children sang, as did a mother who has the voice of an angel, raising money for the Royal British Legion.

Every school has diversity within and beyond its gates, elderly neighbours, local grants to bid for and local businesses to engage. The trick must be to utilize these with integrity and a desire for lasting impact.

Further developments

◆ Create flags for school grounds, but ask stakeholders from your community to contribute a lasting emblem, for celebrating positives within your area. Some examples of these are available via the companion website.

◆ Contact large companies who often have volunteer schemes, but be clear what you need and how this can work for you and the business.

◆ Consider safeguarding guidelines for visitors: if a 'one off' visit and accompanied by a teacher, full CRB clearance is not always necessary. Check with your local authority for guidance.

◆ Religious leaders have out-of-term-time contact with your families, as do Children's Centres. Signpost out-of-hours support and events via your website.

◆ Use Disadvantage Subsidy grants to support vulnerable pupils or children in need. (Try Grants for Schools or National Lottery funding for larger projects, but local councils often have smaller pots of money available for community projects, which reach beyond the school.)

◆ Consider use of local knowledge, first within the school community, by welcoming parents' or governors' links to other organizations.

◆ Use the School website to market who are 'Friends of Our School'.

◆ Encourage sports, charity and voluntary groups to attend or participate in assemblies.

◆ Develop the parent/staff links. Enabling staff and parents to volunteer for a specific event really helps working parents to get involved, without overburdening a few good folk. We have been lucky that under the leadership of a mum, Bev, people have had a personal approach to feel valued and have been given a clear role to perform. This has empowered many and raised funds for the School but also taken the ownership of the vision to the parents. Planning time between Head and Chair outside of meetings is time well spent: to 'iron out' any concerns and plan events a year ahead successfully builds projects around the School diary and avoids overload!

◆ When considering learning opportunities outdoors, don't stop at the School gate. Maths surveys, photographic workshops … there are endless opportunities to extend learning *from* your community.

◆ To ensure development of the Governing Body is with a shared vision, the relationship between Head and chair is crucial. This doesn't mean it is always easy, but there must be a basis of mutual respect and honesty, to unpick issues of discord or concern. My current chair of governors, John, has immense patience, is a good listener and can challenge when necessary. We aim to meet once a week and set aside this time as often as this is realistic. This commitment alone, means he and I communicate as often as I do with my Deputy, such is the impact of his role. Email content is essential in ensuring quick, succinct feedback, when needed.

◆ Perhaps the hardest thing to do is for leaders to stand back, to encourage governors and other stakeholders to take greater responsibility for developments. Again, this does not happen immediately, but in time. To set up an activity and leave the room for it to be led by chair or vice chair can free up debate without an over-reliance on (or dominance by) the Head. In time, due to his work skills, our chair, John, has led training and workshops, and planned notionally with the Head prior to the event, but with him ably supported by his vice chair. This marks the journey of stakeholders from good to outstanding practice by applying the skills of governors to continue the sustainable school.

8 Does Anyone Know Where Lesotho is?: Developing a Global School, Engaging with Schools and Learning Opportunities Overseas

> *When taking up the position of Head at Howe Dell, I had already seen the benefits of international placements on teacher retention and curriculum development. It took 22 years for it to be my turn and it was, to quote a cliché, 'life changing'. I realize so clearly that we are growing global citizens as custodians of this beautiful planet and need to hold this close to our vision, whatever the obstacles.*

When Head of a small school, I was very aware of the benefits of recruiting newly qualified teachers: they were full of enthusiasm, keen to begin their teaching journey and ... they were cheap! My mother was an estate agent running her own business and used to regularly say, if exasperated with her staff, 'I don't pay Ferrari money and expect lawnmowers.' Well ... no one joins the teaching profession to so much as *own* such a vehicle, let alone a salary to maintain it! In comparison, newly qualified teachers are paid lawnmower money, even today, so in return I have always promised Ferrari-style opportunities, in terms of professional development.

During my two headships, 12 staff have been encouraged to learn overseas, to enhance professional development and also to open debate for school improvement, with visits to:

- ◆ Croatia
- ◆ France
- ◆ Denmark
- ◆ Sweden
- ◆ Finland
- ◆ The Gambia
- ◆ Berlin
- ◆ South Africa
- ◆ Brazil

All but the last three were funded through the British Council, remaining projects via Microsoft Innovative Teachers' Forum.

Staff visiting Croatia, with a focus on Gifted and Talented provision, returned with a stronger understanding of our School vision and in fact the opportunities available to children in the UK. Perhaps whilst the beauty of the country and warmth of the welcome had the most lasting impact, staff returned with increased confidence to share how they now valued more the opportunities for extending able pupils in the UK. There was some learning, and some shared agenda, as one school partnered with us proudly demonstrated they too had gained the prestigious Eco Schools Green Flag accreditation. What is perhaps more significant is the fact that both members of staff staff involved in the visit remain at Howe Dell, and have evolved from satisfactory/ good teachers to outstanding teachers. Indeed, one practitioner is our Key Stage 1 leader and ESD Subject Leader, while the other is just returning from maternity leave to run Modern Foreign Languages across the School.

There have been other such opportunities for continued professional development which impact on the teacher as a person, as well as a professional, including our Year 4 teacher visiting France to learn how to teach French, which he continues to use with his classes today. Staff stay longer in organizations where they are valued, their voice is heard and their role is developed. This should never be underestimated by a school leader.

What is the Scandinavian legacy?

Denmark inspired the extended opportunities for learning and, at times, the way in which personalized learning can be tapped via out-of-hours activities. This continues to impact upon philosophy today, in providing exciting and varied childcare from three months to school age, with wrap around care available for nursery children and consistency in leadership and ethos. The children's views for the Breakfast Club and After School Club have adapted ongoing provision including greater use of large-scale art projects and design and sale of fruit cocktails. Bored Year 6 pupils in their last term can have a detrimental impact on overall provision, so encouraging their active participation continues good role models for younger pupils.

The out-of-term play schemes have filled up, largely via word of mouth, with parents adding to evaluations that their children insisted on being booked in for additional sessions, due to the variation of activities, use of outdoors and creative use of skills as diverse as modern foreign language, cookery and ICT. This is very much in line with Danish provision, whilst the risk taking was inspired by Finland. Staff returned in awe of School buildings with no fences and children running off to play in woodland. This is not viable in urban Hatfield, but a spirit of adventure remains, from kite flying to pond dipping to climbing high: sensing one's own limitations.

There was also a real focus on introducing thematic events, known as 'Wonder Days' – a chance to approach basic skills with exciting stimuli including artists, illustrators, actors and inspirational members of our local community. This continues to be central to our approach to learning today and testimony of its impact is best shown by the fact that our Wonder Days have focused on developing literacy skills and engaging whole families in lifelong learning. In the last four years our Level 5+ attainment at Year 6 has gone from 5 per cent to 15 per cent to over 45 per cent. This higher attainment has now been maintained for the third year.

Swedish influence impacted on the design of our Early Years outdoor area: it inspired me and another member of staff to complete further professional study at Masters level about outdoor learning. This transferred to the Howe Dell new build, where a clean canvas for 0–5 outdoor provision, enabled Swedish ideas to be close to our central vision. There needs to be education for parents to ensure that the philosophy of 'There's no such thing as bad weather, just bad clothing' is accepted, and for parents to expect daily free flow to outdoor learning, whatever the forecast!

As a leader, the challenge is knowing when compromise is fine and when to stick to your vision

Albeit a new build is every Head's dream, our delays meant no outdoor shelter was planned from the offset as it was not recognized to have the benefits that it does now. Ironically, the sensitive relationship between heat and light from natural sources caused real issues, with the inclusion of an outdoor shelter with a membrane finally agreed, to still enable the building to work effectively. The challenge can often be ensuring that the clever designers *actually listen* to what is practical in a school setting. It is easy to feel disempowered, but the school leader brings an essential skill set to the table.

Furthermore, having had the experience of a new site with many 'gadgets', the question most important in terms of maintenance is whether they all work alongside one another and what are the costs. I was under the impression these would be minimal for the first year or two, but found warranties would not be honoured unless maintenance agreements were complete. In a building with solar panels and wind turbine, where even the light bulbs don't come from a local hardware store, this is worthy of consideration. Perhaps it's different in northern Europe!

Nevertheless, using Devolved Formula Capital saved from the previous site (spend minimally on a if known to be short term base) large play equipment was bought from sustainable forests and paid for beyond the building scheme. Likewise, for all the advantages of choosing this ethical play equipment, which was tall and abstract and challenging to use (all great strengths in this sterile world of health and safety and sanitized learning!), the number and size of trees planted were reduced due to escalating costs. As a result, there are bids submitted by Howe Dell for many tree planting projects to this day (see www.ecoschools.org.uk for current projects available).

Trees that *were* planted were selected by a working party of parents, staff, pupils and governors who were previously involved in the 'Ground Force Club' – a boy-friendly gardening extra-curricular activity. This gave ownership and responsibility to a group representing our School community, but enabled the decision to be made quickly. It is impractical for everyone to be consulted on every new aspect of school development, hence the role of the school leader is to spread the decision making to be inclusive, yet effective.

The site has been reviewed by many professional and amateur visitors over the last three years, but the Finland impact of no boundaries and risk in learning outdoors was most evident when Year 6 were asked to risk assess the new play apparatus. I was walking around the site somewhat absorbed in Ofsted preparations at the end of our second day, when I was called across by the children: the whole class were straddled at different heights on the wonderful climbing structure and, as I walked up, in unison they shouted,

'1, 2, 3 … THANK YOU!!'

So Finland had impact on our provision, and northern Europe generally continues to be a place of inspiration. Visits from schools in Finland have been reciprocated, the teachers taking on board our ESD curriculum and pastoral support. Therefore, as in the best partnerships, learning is symbiotic.

Learning FROM Africa, rather than just giving TO developing countries

Through links with the University of Hertfordshire, two staff had the chance to visit the Gambia, and the learning in and beyond the classroom has impacted on assemblies, themed weeks and the diversity strand of our curriculum, especially since by relocating from July to September 2007 our ethnic minority percentage rose from 10–11 per cent to 30 per cent. This continues to be an ever diverse learning resource for us all, as we gain greater under-standing of a constantly expanding list of cultures and communities. Moreover, seeing how school gardens in the Gambia produced food and necessary medicines for their community, made the organization of allotments and rotation of crops less whimsical back at School! The appointment of a Grounds Co-ordinator with a teaching background was essential in whole site development. This needed credibility with strong willed colleagues, and energy and passion for outdoors: Ginny had all of these.

So where does Lesotho fit in? Through the teaching awards I had an invitation to apply to Microsoft to be a judge at a global ICT competition: the Worldwide Innovative Teachers' Forum. To this day, I am unsure whether I was successful as my letter ended by saying that I valued the chance for staff to learn from and apply skills gained overseas, but the furthest I'd ever gone for profes-sional development was eastern England! Perhaps they felt sorry for me – my young staff members were protective that my confidence with PowerPoint and editing DVDs would not suffice in this arena! Thankfully, the role of judge was not focusing on an 'ICT gizmo and gadget show', but a celebration of outstanding teaching and learning. It was truly humbling. The creativity and determination shown by teachers, notably from developing countries, to provide excellence often against adversity brought tears to my eyes.

Extract of press release for teaching awards

Other outcomes from the trip were life changing. Our curriculum is already award winning through Teaching Awards and elsewhere, but the skills I learnt in Brazil have been shared with staff and are now impacting on delivery in the classroom (e.g. Wordle, but with braille added as an evaluation tool, or Word Wall to collate staff ideas on how we might best use Nintendo DS in Basic Skills delivery). The 21st Century Skills first seen in Brazil have been used with my leadership team to review short-, medium- and long-term curriculum development.

More importantly, the young teacher from Lesotho who had no electricity in her classroom – and raised money by selling oranges to use the nearest towns' internet cafe as her ICT suite, made a lasting impression. I was so inspired by her work that I convinced her to come to the UK – not as an act of charity, but for my staff to learn from her.

The teacher who won the Educators' Choice prestigious award had breakfast with me on the last morning and I told her I would like her to come to the UK, to share her story and her teaching with staff and pupils at my School and beyond. (I had no idea how I would do this, but knew it *had* to happen!) Moliehi Sekese, with what I now know to be her natural charm and enthusiasm, was keen to explore that possibility and a friendship was born.

November 2010

How to pace change and innovation

- ◆ Returning to School, an overview of the visit to Brazil was shared in assembly, through themes set prior to my visit. I was sensitive to the fact that in mid-November, staff were focused on ongoing assessments, with Christmas plays and concerts looming: I did not want to 'kill off my staff' with my excitement and new ideas.
- ◆ Therefore, I booked Microsoft to come to Howe Dell in the New Year and waited for the whole site INSET in January to share lasting impressions, clarifying their future impact on our organization. (The last thing even the kindest colleagues want to see is an endless stream of holiday snaps!)
- ◆ It was during this INSET that I showed how the new technology could be incorporated into future training and how creativity would be enhanced by this.
- ◆ Plans to book Moliehi's visit began on my return, impacting on nothing at School except my blood pressure! The process was far more difficult than I had thought, as most international airlines were not happy with her ticket being bought by me for a visit of a week without work permits, albeit we could demonstrate that this was an educational visit for the benefit of children and staff in both countries. Thankfully Virgin Atlantic made the trip possible and she arrived as planned, funded initially by consultancy money raised through presentations offsite, but later, due to the impact for adults and children, we justified this as a teaching and learning project, through the School budget share.
- ◆ Microsoft and 'powers that be' heard of this venture and this resulted in the week beginning with a 9 a.m. whole School assembly, sharing Moliehi's indigenous plants project, resulting in follow-up lessons on Africa, gardens (sharing our aims to develop learning outdoors) and ICT.

◆ By 10.30 a.m. on the same morning, we were on our way to the QEII Hall, Westminster, where this young teacher gave a presentation to the World Forum for Learning and Technology. Within the audience of 800 were representatives of the World Bank and 57 ministers representing over 1 billion of the World's children.
◆ Her dignity and passion for teaching and learning shone and she was one of three delegates introduced to various dignitaries including the then British Prime Minister Gordon Brown, who referred to her in his speech.

On our way home, Moliehi chatted about her day with strangers on the Tube: the impact of this sparkling personality in rush hour humdrum was electric:

Moliehi: When I met the Prime Minister earlier today, his name is Mr Gordon Brown, you know …

Commuter: Bad luck love! [returning to book]

*Moliehi: No! You don't understand! He is a **good** man and he shook my hand …*

*Me: Yes he did Moliehi, but perhaps more importantly **you** shook **his** hand!*

Extract from journal, January 2010

The week went all too quickly and children and staff gained an insight into Africa that at times was heartbreaking.

◆ Five Maths books for 51 children in Moliehi's class.
◆ Journeys to the town to photocopy, not popping into a staffroom.
◆ Twenty-four orphans out of 51 classmates due to AIDS.
◆ The lack of colour in a classroom with chalk and chalkboard.

However, there were positives, too.

◆ The ownership of the children in their learning: 'They RAN to the river to collect heavy rocks to make their garden.'
◆ The generosity of staff and families as gifts of crayons, pencils, stickers came flooding in – not to mention clothes.
◆ The most poignant gift was from Nadia who had £50 birthday money: we converted these into books that took six months to arrive.
◆ When the visit was over, Moliehi's small suitcase was accompanied

by a further large case, the 32 lb luggage restriction was doubled – and some 74 kg due to the gifts. This obviously caused a problem at check-in and, despite the sympathetic stewardesses, we seemed to have met an insurmountable obstacle. I asked to see a manager and basically turned Terminal 3 into an assembly, as I told Moliehi's story as she unpacked her case. Airport staff and strangers were tearful as the manager agreed to take the luggage, if we packed it into smaller containers. We left to cheers and claps! God bless human kindness and Virgin Atlantic.

Back at School, prior to Moliehi's visit I had quietly spoken to my Year 6 teacher about submitting a project he had already done with his children to Microsoft. One lasting impression was how good some of the work in our own School was: we often work at such a pace that we do not always stop to celebrate. Simon had four days, including a weekend, to convert the current project into a format that would be compatible for the Innovative Teachers' UK finals. He knew this time would be paid back in kind, but was motivated by a scent of opportunity. Not only did he reach the top four, being one of first two primary school to represent Microsoft UK, but in March 2010 he came third in his category for Europe of 150 projects. This meant Howe Dell was represented at the Worldwide Innovative Teachers' Forum, not with me as a judge this time, but the work of some talented children from Howe Dell who were inspired by one of our outstanding teachers.

The impact continues, as Simon has seen some ideas in Europe which are now being modified to apply in our School. He has also presented at two county conferences and, without doubt, the use of ICT has been instrumental in supporting the best SATS results our School has ever acquired.

Microsoft representatives have come in to show our staff software that I could have introduced, but the credence of the training was heightened by Microsoft's involvement, further endorsed by each teacher being given half a day's non-contact time *to practise from the software which will be most relevant to their professional development*. It is vital when giving training with ICT that teachers have a chance to choose their next steps, dependent on confidence and prior experience, just as a differentiated lesson outcome is expected for children. By inviting non-teaching staff to the training has impacted beyond the School day: in the After School Club in the summer term when some Key Stage 2 pupils did a PowerPoint on 'Let's Get Cooking' for our whole School assembly, a child was overheard saying, 'Let's put Auto Collage into the final slide as our plenary.'

And Moliehi Sekese? She continues to teach in Lesotho, is in touch via email when technology and time allows, and all of her students passed their national tests. Moreover, my next project is to take a teacher, governor, teaching assistant and child with me to Lesotho. How? I am not sure, but it will be done – as our continued mission to grow global citizenship unfolds.

Further developments

- Easy ICT Auto Collage for combined photos – brilliant for year books or calendars.
- British Council – will receive bids from groups of teachers which encourage learning from and with teachers from overseas.
- Exciting outdoor equipment from sustainable sources: Timberplay (timberplay.co.uk) were excellent.
- Nintendo DS – relatively cheap and great for learning basic skills in Maths, especially for boys.
- Likewise, our Nintendo Wii with games linked to competition and mental maths (darts and bowling) are great motivators for developing mental maths.
- If looking for links with schools, especially in developing countries, choose a topic to which both can contribute equally – hence our gardens theme encouraged shared learning. DO NOT assume developed countries know best!
- If staff are engaged in a big project, give time in lieu as a thank you and ensure food expenses and travel are fully paid – in my experience staff will go the extra mile if they:
  - ✓ feel valued;
  - ✓ have the credit for the work and resulting glory.
- Use local press and beyond to celebrate projects.
- School website is an excellent recruitment tool, so ensure outcomes of such projects and impact for school, pupils and staff is celebrated.
- Avoid an 'us and them' culture by inviting all staff and governors to staff meetings relevant to them. This might need a direct prompt in some cases but has especially extended teaching assistants' ability to teach whole classes and link governors' engagement with particular curriculum areas.
- Review the partnership for 21st Century Skills (see partnership

for 21st Century Skills) model as a leadership task for school improvement, to establish what is already in place, and what is possible in the short-, medium- and long-term. This was useful as a planning tool for reviewing curriculum development.

◆ As a matter of policy, all staff and governors are given staff meeting themes in advance of a term beginning, so that opportunities to 'dip into' onsite training is encouraged.

9 | Multi-Faith, Multi-Ethnic and EAL Pupils

An earnest 10 year old arrived at Howe Dell mid Year 5, with fathomless eyes, a shy smile and minimal English. Within a term she was popular with pupils and, staff adding fluent English to her stock of three other languages. She excelled at Mathematics but continued to find Science vocabulary a challenge. This child applied herself confidently to the life of the School, yet sadly her family did not settle so easily into Hatfield, nor indeed the UK. They returned to Eastern Europe due to homesickness. A clear lesson in how inclusion must mean real community cohesion, building links for whole families, if it is to stand a chance. What is the School context?

Over two years, our numbers on roll steadily grew, with a slight increase of ethnic minority pupils extending to 10 per cent. However, by relocating a mile and a half to the new site, we opened our doors after a six-week summer holiday to further increased numbers on roll, but ethnicity beyond 'White British pupils' stood at above 30 per cent and rising. This was a wonderful opportunity, not only to encourage the whole staff to learn more about diversity but to learn from the children and their families themselves. It became a cornerstone of our School curriculum, which can be accessed via the School website.

It really wasn't that difficult; with transferable planning to other organizations as follows:

◆ Children new to the School were linked to current pupils who spoke their mother tongue.
◆ Greater emphasis was used, especially in Foundation Stage, to utilize all languages at times such as snack time as well as timetabled curriculum.

♦ Parents were welcome into School as part of the children's induction, often resulting in us learning much more about the rich culture from whence these families had grown up.

Finding a real need for parental engagement within the School

By ensuring Themed Weeks encouraged parent-led workshops, *alongside* teachers for support, to pitch the content appropriate to the age and stage of the audience, mothers arrived first with gifts of food or examples of crafts such as embroidery and henna painting. This later developed to include dads and grandads talking about their childhood memories and being role models for reading, which inspired the young audience. The way in which this is organized, the building of individual relationships, all bear fruit in cascading a strongly positive message about engagement to the wider parent body.

Caleb and Mum enjoy an intro-duction to henna hand painting together.
This has since become a regular attraction at School fetes.

Engaging dads

When we were assessed by our county council for our Foundation Stage provision, advisers celebrated the engagement of a particularly challenging Polish boy through the involvement of his father, a benefit which was far reaching for the dynamics of the learning environment for all. Other engagement strategies which might encourage a leader to value people within the School community as a resource include:

◆ A father who had been unemployed was encouraged to volunteer in Early Years and later became a permanent member of staff.
◆ A long term MSA (midday supervisor) who was once reticent about training also began working in our newly formed After School Club and later became a key developer of extended services through his work in Breakfast Club and Holiday Play schemes. He was also a 'real hit' in Day Care.

Extending this 'men in a traditionally female dominated environment' starts initially with a willingness to contribute and it grows from there. For many of our children, the strong male role model is invaluable, especially in reaffirming emotional wellbeing. This is recognized by parents, as evident in a thank you note which was published via our School newsletter:

'… I just wanted to express how delighted we are about my son's involvement in Breakfast and After School clubs. He enjoys the large amount of activities offered by both clubs and always has something to report on his time with you. I am always amazed at how organized and well planned the activities are. Safeguarding is clearly of great importance to planning and staff, as it is evident when I pick Thomas up.

   I also would like to mention how helpful and friendly all the staff are; they are always smiling and happy to help. My son is very fond of Mr Carpenter who is quite exceptional with the children; all your staff have very high expectations …'

Be receptive to ideas from the community: an example

During a conversation with a local curate, Susan Marsh, at the Old Rectory Drive building, she mooted an idea about a blessing for the new site. I loved the concept but wanted to make it fully inclusive: Howe Dell was a community school and if we were going to do it, it needed to be a multi-faith act of collective worship. The next step was discussing the idea with teachers and governors who were politely keen at yet another idea, but all asked the same questions – 'How do we do it? What does it look like?' My answer was simple … I had no idea, but felt we ought to use the community within our School at the time of transition to establish the vision and content.

This was enhanced as a shared idea by involving not just our curate, but the Methodist minister who was a resident of the estate and new to our Governing Body. Using interested parties known to the School is the foundation stone. Next, I spoke to the Religious Education subject leader during her performance management in September, suggesting it would be an excellent professional development opportunity for her to co-ordinate this, with ongoing support from me. This was a scaffolded leadership opportunity for a colleague which clearly demonstrated the opportunities of a subject *leader*, as opposed to co-ordinator.

By this time, there was sufficient trust between Nikki and me for her to know she would not be abandoned and whilst this had initially been mentioned in June 2007, we scheduled time to make this an event of note for some point in the summer term of 2008. It is vital for something very new, especially when involving closely held personal beliefs, that time and attention to detail is given to encourage ownership of the event by the majority. Also, negotiation around the early vision must be very much part of the planning process.

The proposal went public via a School newsletter, inviting people to contribute ideas or suggest spokespeople for key religions. This opens the possibility of engaging a wider community through the School's extended links. It also involved many face-to-face conversations before and after School, talking to parents, seeking views and 'twisting the occasional arm'. Welcome surprises also occurred, such as a member of my Children's Centre steering group offering to represent Bahai thinking, with a PowerPoint aimed at encouraging the children to reflect; and the previous County Adviser for Religious Education agreeing to represent Judaism (and tick the box for Herts County Council at the event!).

As mentioned previously, having set the wheels in motion, the biggest challenge for a leader is then to let go and enable *(not disable)* those you've encouraged to steer the event. Nikki and our School governor kept the itinery close to their chest, saying they wanted me to enjoy it for what it was: it remains the highlight of the School opening, beyond the Royal visit and first day, due to its simplicity and a certain message of hope and aspiration.

If encouraging parental involvement, wrap it up in pupil-based activity, as parents are more likely to come along, if nagged by children!

In the build-up to the Multi-Faith Act of Collective Worship, we had a themed week of international dance, storytelling and extended opportunities for speaking and listening as well as writing. Funding is not endless, but if there is a wider community engagement, Lottery, local council and Grants for Schools, as well as donations of raffle prizes from local businesses, can all be sources of revenue. Furthermore, schools remain places of learning, so publishing aims of the event, embedded in developing key skills, heightens its value.

Members of the community came for an international evening of shared music, food and culture – 200 people attended. Since then, a local residents' group offer an annual event entitled 'From Hatfield with Love' which runs independently of the school, but uses the building free of charge. This makes the long-term plan more sustainable. Including an evening or weekend event makes the school accessible for adult learners who work full time.

What made the event 'multi-faith'?

◆ It began with Susan, whose initial idea prompted this wonderful act of collective worship. She talked about how beautiful, but fragile, our world was. We as an eco School have a chance to shape the thoughts and actions of those near and afar in making it strong and safe. Our Religious Education Adviser then told the story of Genesis pictorially and Nikki's children danced.

◆ Our Bahai representative used a PowerPoint with music entitled 'One World', with stunning images of children from around the globe and occasional inspirational messages. He is not a teacher and when the children first started to wriggle, I watched nervously from the sidelines thinking he was losing them. To my delight, I then realized that from 4-year-olds to Year 6, they weren't disengaged at all. In fact the children were using body percussion independently and building a rhythm in response to the music … even more powerful was the whisper from the back of the hall which eventually became a mantra as unprompted, they read 'One World' again and again. The Bahai faith may not be present within every school community, but any Buddhist reflection or focal point could provide a similar opportunity to reflect. Encouraging children to listen and respond to a range of music through assembly can empower a response to add to the spirituality.

Work around challenges, rather than build walls to respond to problems

The remaining challenge throughout the planning had been Islam. Our only Muslim member of staff was unable to recommend an available imam to add to the ceremony, and I was concerned about causing offence. What actually happened could never have been planned in a spider diagram or in a strategic meeting.

A grandmother of a Year 1 pupil and regular volunteer in School was Muslim and she confirmed via her brother, who was an Imam, that in the absence of such a religious leader, someone else could say some prayers: man or woman. I held my breath as this petite and dignified lady took the floor and began her prayer in Arabic. She was flanked by her granddaughter and another Muslim child. As she quietly spoke on her knees, the School craned to see her tiny frame, in hushed awe. As she spoke, the two children by her side translated the words into English, culminating in the announcement that as we celebrated the creation of our School, mosques elsewhere in the world had added Howe Dell to their prayers that day.

There were other wonderful moments during the service, including a long-term friend from the Hare Krishna community finishing a day of teaching in the School with a story encouraging pupil participation. Prayers and songs were shared and it remains a powerful part of our School's history. Since then, we have opened our building to a Polish church through the use of satellite-linked services, we host courses for members of the community to learn English and our children from ethnic minorities thrive.

Where do you start?

It doesn't have to be a huge event. Like so many successes, projects can start small and grow through their own momentum.

◆ Welcome parents into class first, then later assembly, to share hobbies, interests, food.

◆ Use assemblies as a chance to develop empathy between cultures by role playing rites of passage or having parents and children share special events.

◆ Consider how this can be planned as an annual programme by including in long-term planning processes.

◆ Try offering food as part of parent-teacher consultations, especially if made by the children. Our curry nights meant more parents came for longer and the event seemed more welcoming and social. It also raised funds for future projects!

◆ Have photographs on display around the school reaffirming the value of diversity, with images and artefacts from children's homes.

◆ To engage with parents, encourage a broader involvement by seeking out key parents. 'Your son says you have started an allotment – I'd love you to talk to some children about that.'

◆ Give extended notice of key events, so that working parents have a chance to get involved.

◆ Rather than an evening event, offer a Saturday morning project through a shared focus, e.g. healthy eating, gardening or 'strictly ballroom – dads and daughters', as suggested by a child, following the success of *Strictly Come Dancing*.

◆ Remember, diversity needs to bridge the generations: invite local old people's home residents to school events, but visit there too with children. A local resident who lived through the Blitz has lots of stories to enthral young people, many of whom do not have an extended family.

◆ If all else fails? Shamelessly tout for parental involvement! This text message did the trick: *'Come on Mums and Dads! Surely you have something of interest in your lives other than us children! Tell us about it please!' (From the Children's Council).*

As a result, for our Healthy Schools Week, we had dads sharing football and fishing, mums sharing Indian cookery and card making, and one Traveller mum celebrating how her family had lived on the road and brought wedding dresses to show, to name but a few examples.

The impact was huge. Each parent was praised in the newsletter and received a certificate in assembly, accompanied by their child – and we've never looked back. A local fishing club has even donated equipment and time for our families to learn a new outdoor sport at a local amenity.

Where did this richness come from? *It was there already*, just underused, with more recent examples of engagement being religious groups led by parents, and donations of flower arrangements and photography from other parents who have returned to education to extend their own skills.

Use self-evaluation to reinforce what is working well, and next steps

There are a number of tools on the companion website, but welcoming students or researchers into school can give greater insight into provision.

◆ Hosting a trainee Head via the NPQH programme, which any school categorized as good or better can offer through NCSL, I wanted to return to the issue of that multi-faith, multi ethnic school, which I believe we are successfully growing (www.nationalcollege.org.uk).

◆ The host school must provide five days' training with a clear focus project for the trainee, gaining £500 for the school as a consultancy fee. Commitment of Head and other leaders is essential in the success of the project and to meet the aspiration of growing leadership beyond our immediate place of work.

◆ We do not have *one* large 'ethnic' group; we have many small groups from all parts of the globe who are new to Hatfield. They need to overcome English not being their first language in order to gain from the learning we offer. We also have ever increasing groups of families who enrich our provision and teach us to be better facilitators of an inclusive community.

◆ It doesn't always happen in 'shafts of light' and huge public events. Sometimes the quiet 'drip feed' of trust is what is needed over a long period of time, to achieve what two years ago I would never have believed. Perhaps the most recent example of this is how a family with two deaf parents are beginning to engage with Children's Centre staff in developing play and social interaction for their hearing child. Suddenly English as an additional language has a whole new meaning.

Tangible outcomes

◆ The placement of our NPQH trainee Head gave me chance to revisit this area, but through an outsider reviewing:

✓   our data;
✓   interviews with EAL children and parents;
✓   questionnaires from staff;
✓   Close collaboration with our INCO and Head.

◆   She was given many opportunities to see Howe Dell in action to extend her understanding. As a result, she phoned me as her placement ended, frustrated that not much had been achieved. Impressed at her honesty and tenacity, we talked about what had arisen from her research. It appeared that there was no 'Holy Grail', no one step solution, but what was clear was the overriding view of parents and children that they didn't feel they were treated differently due to EAL. Now I call that quite an outcome! Extracts of the research below, highlight the value of an outside view on what is new and challenging:
'None of the pupils felt that they were any different to any of the other children in their class.'
'Overwhelmingly, the single factor that contributed most to pupil progress was the ethos *of the school. All children stated that they* enjoyed *coming to school and felt equal in class.'*

Further Developments

◆   A Multi-Faith Act of Collective Worship could be used to open part of a new build or to draw attention to a project or initiative in school. If parents know the children are involved in some way, they are more likely to attend.
◆   Whole school assemblies focusing on celebrating success in the broadest context, acknowledges interests and experiences of children and their families within and beyond school. Examples might include:
✓   A first Communion.
✓   An Indian dance.
✓   A parent has run the marathon for a particular charity and why.
✓   Fundraising and school awards.
✓   Don't miss an opportunity!
◆   As the school budget allows, increase resources that can be used in RE, History, PSHCE and in assemblies. One useful website is www.articlesoffaith.co.uk.
◆   If language or literacy barriers exist, borrow a visualizer from a

local college or secondary school, to enlarge artefacts and photos to heighten the impact of their worth. This was used successfully for some Traveller workshops led by parents.

- Publish Celebrating Success Policy – see School website for an example.
- EAL project – talk to children and parents, use some of the Ofsted questions from questionnaires to reports. Results from the project can inform the SEF in transferrable language.
- Encourage parents to come to school with a specific purpose – it's like a 'golden ticket' making the invitation personal and heightening the value of what they bring.
- Look at the data: gender/subject all linked to prescribed 'vulnerable groups' so that intervention can be targeted. See EAL and behaviour pyramids available on line which is part of our inclusion policy.
- Remember to use skills and knowledge of those around you but also enable middle managers, and HLTAs subject leaders a chance to shine, scaffolding support so that success is assured, but still earned.
- Encourage team working to include governors: they have so many skills and to use these well is better than spreading the involvement too thinly.
- Work with those you know understand the vision of what you need first. However, sometimes by giving a high-profile project to someone who is a strong critical friend can also raise their credibility and develop your professional relationship.

Section 3: Reaching the Tallest Branches

10 | Rewriting the Curriculum: Embedding an Education for Sustainable Development (ESD)

'And what target shall we put for professional development this year?' This was the question – asked of all teachers and leadership team members in the first year of being at our new School – and the focus was clear: we needed to share good practice and demonstrate how it worked with people who had the creditability of using it every day. And so our plan to share our ECO curriculum with a wider audience became central to the agenda.

I didn't wake up one morning and have a Eureka moment, 'Lets host a conference for 80 delegates, to set our curriculum up as exemplary practice!' The journey to that point was long and shared. It was supported by expertise within and beyond the School and was at a time when a team believed in a vision sufficiently to be prepared to 'Give It a Go!'

Where do you start?

There have been many documents and programmes to support curriculum development, with changes in the political arena swaying what might or might not be the 'best way'. As a leader, it is important to view the curriculum as a vessel, steered by professionals, on a course which might at times venture into the unknown, but learning and opportunity remain clear compass bearings.

Five years ago, as a new Head who was developing behaviour management, organizational procedures and the vision of the School almost daily, it was a relief to find an early draft of our current curriculum in the previous Head's office. It evolved from a key principle that our world was precious and needed to be nurtured, for future generations:

> The vision of education for sustainable development is a world where everyone has the opportunity to benefit from quality education and learn the values, behaviour and lifestyles required for a sustainable future and for positive societal transformation.
> United Nations decade of Education for Sustainable Development, 2004

It was unfinished and erred too much on the side of safety and security to be inspirational, albeit the potential was there. (It relied heavily on QCA topics, as this was the security blanket of the previous regime.) When implemented, over time, it had dramatic

Green Shoots
A gift for all delegates attending the Eco Conference was a home-grown sapling of willow from Howe Dell, planted in a recycled container. This was a project from our After School Club.

impact on the attainment and progress of our children and the attitudes held by stakeholders. Hence, the final 'leap of faith' took place in a reworking of the original plan. This is available through the School website and is endorsed by two University of Hertfordshire reports, both also available via the School website.

> 'What impact has the curriculum had internally and beyond the School's doors? The research data shows that the ESD principles embedded within the curriculum and ethos of the School are having a tangible impact on attitude and lifestyle of pupils, parents and staff alike. This impact is particularly apparent among the pupils who have become agents for change for ESD principles within their own families and neighbourhoods.'
>
> University of Hertfordshire, 2009

Nurturing 'green shoots'

In every school, the early signs of change and improvement can be easily overlooked or even destroyed by too much hot-housing, which can make the end product tasteless and lacking in credibility. Honestly, I am sure moments were lost in the pace of change at Howe Dell. However, what survived the time of transition had strong roots and a shared belief that cemented the 'young saplings' of curriculum design, which have since helped rejuvenate learning in and beyond the School.

The curriculum at an early stage had considerable input from John Burden, an adviser of Geography and Citizenship in a past life, who I'd worked closely with when I was County Adviser for PSHCE. It was based on seven key concepts and attempted to thread these across the primary curriculum. Stephen Sterling drafted these seven key concepts which help us identify opportunities for ESD. These themes were used in Ofsted's ESD 'First Steps Report' in 2003. These are the foundations for ESD at Howe Dell and have been shared across Hertfordshire and been award winning beyond our county.

Key Concept 1 – Interdependence
Understanding how people, the environment and the economy are inextricably linked at all levels from local to global.
For example, ecosystems; aid and trade/fair trade issues; impact of oil price changes; impact of foot and mouth and other epidemics affecting animals or humans; impact of changing tourism fashions.

Key Concept 2 – Citizenship and stewardship
Recognizing the importance of taking individual responsibility and action to ensure the world is a better place.
For example, taking greater responsibility for the School and local environment – involvement in eco Schools and School council; tending the School garden; avoiding waste in resource use (for example, water and construction materials) and energy supplies.

Key Concept 3 – Needs and rights of future generations
Understanding our own basic needs and the implications for the needs of future generations of actions taken today.
For example, for food, shelter, health, education and a safe and secure environment.

Key Concepts 4 – Diversity
Respecting and valuing both human diversity – cultural, social and economic – and biodiversity.
For example, human diversity can be respected and valued through Art, Music, RE, Geography; and biodiversity would include the study of ecology and ecosystems in Science and Geography.

Key Concept 5 – Quality of life
Acknowledging that global equity and justice are essential elements of sustainability and that basic needs must be met universally.
For example, becoming more aware that inequalities in the quality of life can vary locally and globally.

Key Concept 6 – Sustainable change
Understanding that resources are finite and that this has implications for people's lifestyles and for commerce and industry.
For example, in the use of energy resources, fuel and consumables; packaging; food and farming.

Key Concept 7 – Uncertainty and precaution
Acknowledging that there are a range of possible approaches to sustainability and that situations are constantly changing, indicating a need for flexibility and lifelong learning.
For example, through the study of topical ESD issues using debates, discussion, role play, drama and decision-making exercises.

Partly as a demonstration to value prior input from staff who had been working at the School for some time, during a dramatic time of change, this document was 'dusted off' and introduced as our new mantra. The directive was non-negotiable: 'This is what we stand for and we're all going to use this for a year.' The agreement being:

♦ That good and bad, the document which had dominated so many previous staff meetings, but had never been used *would be trialled*.

♦ As with many projects to follow, the expectation was that all would follow this directive – and so they did, with a positive and open mind.

♦ With the exception of anything that was unsafe or not age appropriate, in which case content was modified, this document was indeed followed doggedly, evaluated constantly and where ideas or topics did not work, they were annotated with suggested replacement content.

This was a slow process to begin with, as I had no Deputy, temporary staff, an NQT and the new but good experienced teachers. Teachers were expected to include ESD key concepts in their weekly- and medium-term planning, highlighting these in green. I visited classrooms weekly to sign off the planning and see it in the context of 'live lessons' as well as regular lesson observations. Developing a culture of regular planning review *within the classroom context* brings an openness to the sudden arrival of senior leaders in classrooms for short periods of time and an invaluable insight into a developing ethos within the School. I led by example, keeping my door open unless in a confidential meeting, and classrooms followed suit. This approach needs to be clear in performance management policies or in the Staff Handbook.

By the end of the first year, our staffing was more stable; teachers who had been at the School prior to my headship and new staff were beginning to develop their skills and their belief in themselves as an innovative team. It was then appropriate for subject leaders (renamed and rebranded from 'Curriculum Co-ordinators' with bulging files of policies, but little experience of curriculum development or leadership) to be given the 'eco green light': 'You are the experts – collate all the annotated plans for your subject and propose the Howe Dell Curriculum Phase 2'. The importance of subject leaders in seizing ownership of ESD in their specialist field was key and followed the findings of Ofsted in 2002 who reported:

For many of the pupils interviewed in the schools visited, the profile of ESD is raised when it becomes an integral part of the curriculum. Where heads of department or subject co-ordinators review and, where necessary, revise their schemes of work to include opportunities to promote ESD, this reinforces a greater understanding of the key concepts and continues to develop positive attitudes and values towards sustainability issues across the whole school.

Ofsted, *One Small Step*, 2003, p. 6

The second year resulted in greater ownership of this curriculum, yet a continued rigour in core subject assessment or 'Basic Skills'. We were in the bottom 5 per cent in the country for attainment and my inheritance included a 30 per cent difference between passive girls and active boys at Key Stage 2 in Maths. We still monitor rigorously to this day to target passive girl learners at Howe Dell.

With the interest of Hertfordshire University researching the impact on staff, parents, pupils and governors of our ESD curriculum, I recognized that we needed the credibility of some assessment procedures to demonstrate tracking and evaluation of the children's learning journey in ESD. This tool took a huge amount of work from John Burden and our newly appointed ESD Subject Leader, Chris Stewart, alongside input from all staff. The fact that this continued to be led strategically by me and co-ordinated through staff training was key, to maintain focus, but the handover to subject leaders in that second year gave a clear message: 'I trust you to make the right decision for your subject; you are best placed to wear the mantle of expert.' This is available via the companion website.

Meanwhile, the school self-evaluation forms for each subject recognized general school improvement, as well as the enrichment provided by ESD. The inclusion of ESD across the curriculum and its profile in school development is evident in the extract below, from the document drafted by the Literacy subject leader in 2009:

What are the strengths of the teaching that have the greatest impact on learners' progress?

◆ ESD-rich lessons, using relevant and engaging stimuli.
◆ Range of strategies used to stimulate and motivate pupils.
◆ Thorough planning and well structured lessons.
◆ Assessment for learning led well by Deputy – improved independence and evidence of progress since September 2008.
◆ Teacher with consultancy experience in Literacy now very much

upper KS2 based, aiding communication and impacting on some staff confidence across different writing genres.
♦ As well as intervention strategies using the skills of teaching assistants and targeted groups at KS2 benefitting from consultancy input, application for 1:1 tuition has also been sought.
♦ Assessment Manager 7 is proving to be an effective means of focusing assessment on analysis for Head and subject leaders.
♦ Raised profile of writing across the school.
♦ Well-trained TAs provide teachers and pupils with good support.
♦ Under-achievers are identified early from termly distribution sheets and intervention programmes put into place across the school.

This was a highly empowering time for the staff and a time of dramatic change in ethos and provision. So much so, that I brought in a mock Ofsted to see how we were doing, not so much as to check on what they were doing, *but to ensure someone was checking on me!* Having strong accountability is essential to avoid empire building and egocentricity at a massive time of change!

The impact of the curriculum was evaluated by Hertfordshire University prior to us moving to the new site and recognized the value of what we had created: it was transferrable. We had created something which was of worth beyond Howe Dell.

Two days after moving to the Runway site, Ofsted came calling – another chapter perhaps, or maybe just therapy for those involved! The curriculum was praised, albeit the site did not have more than a third of our facilities available and we were still using taxis to get staff into work due to ongoing building work. As a result, the next phase of curriculum development was ready: publishing hard copies of the curriculum for all Hertfordshire schools and launching it electronically via the School and county website. The endorsement and encouragement from Hertfordshire County Council was invaluable in getting our curriculum creditability. From the interest in the new site and via website interest in the curriculum, we were inundated with requests for visits and training. It soon became apparent that this needed to be managed long term. Hence, Visitors' Days on the last Friday of every month were introduced, giving:

♦ teaching and non-teaching staff extended opportunities to share their work;
♦ pupils the chance to lead tours and speak with authority on ESD curriculum and facilities at Howe Dell;

- our engagement with community extending from local, national and international representation (the ESD visitors log is now collated annually as evidence towards community cohesion).

What prompts might suggest a curriculum event has potential in any School?

At Howe Dell, requests for exemplar lessons, resources and visits to other schools were soon to become unmanageable, unless it was led by us. Hence the focus in everyone's performance management to cascade the impact of Howe Dell provision to a wider audience, as a target for professional development.

- Linking it to performance management meant it was a shared focus, with many colleagues being equal stakeholders in its success.
- In any good or better school, there are examples of good practice which could be shared via publishing or through an advertised event. The difference is that not many schools have the courage to do this.
- At a time of reduced budgets one considers the validity of a course and added cost of supply, and I do believe that sharing good practice through partnership working is the way forward. Indeed, this does not just have to be through a consortia of local schools, albeit that can be a start, with each school contributing a workshop for shared INSET, but also through Teaching Awards, NCSL and the Eastern Leadership Centre. In this way, partnerships have evolved with excellent practice in Nottingham, Essex and Africa!
- Use an INSET day to visit another setting and see it 'live'. Evaluating specifically will stop staff just coming back with a 'wish list of resources' but also value what you already do well.
- If an INSET day is not relevant, then take a small group representing different areas of your organization, including caretaker and governor representation.
- Staff need quality time to plan, so as not to undermine the thinking and preparation time necessary to do such an event properly. Hence an INSET day was allocated to planning and the themes of each workshop agreed to ensure:
    - ✓ Pairs of staff could plan and present workshops which have as broad a perspective as possible into provision.

- ✓ Consideration of site facilities (for those embarking on building projects and Children's Centre/Extended Services provision) reinforced the raised profile of non-teaching leaders.
- ✓ Our children were asked to sign up to be tour guides if Children's Council representatives (all of whom were Year 6) or Year 4 and above if Eco Squad members. 23 children arrived in School uniform during half-term to lead tours, and some even joined me, ESD subject leader and others on a panel for a *Question Time*-styled interview session.

Let's go public! This is now good enough to share: remember, every school needs to find 'a marketable gem' (unique selling point!)

To plan the conference, we liaised with Hertfordshire County Council so they were aware of the event and could publicize it. This also prevented duplication with county-led events, but months' notice needs to be given. I created flyers to be distributed to every school, and costings were gauged on costs for county training, but reduced as it was in-house. I contacted a North London Healthy Schools adviser I knew vaguely through a shared colleague, and she looked at the material and was so impressed that she pledged to pay for any subject leader from the Borough of Enfield to attend. Some of our guests from previous Visitors' Days also sent staff. The marketing was specific and whilst ambitious in approach, focused upon what we were confident in delivering, as evident in our introduction available via our School website, and shown below.

ECO CONFERENCE

Date:
Time:
Following the successful completion of the first purpose-built eco school in Britain, and due to demand, Howe Dell is hosting an eco conference to:

- ◆ *Launch the Eco Curriculum created with the support of Hertfordshire County Council. A copy will be sent to Hertfordshire primary schools in the New Year.*

Provide practical seminars led by teachers on planning and resources, showing how ESD can be an integral part of current practice, not another 'bolt on' extra.
- *Tour of the unique site including wind turbine, solar, photovoltaic panels and explanation of our first-in-the-world heating system.*
- *Opportunity to buy eco resources and network with local and national contacts.*
- *Chance to hear from current pupils how pupil voice has shaped a school of the future.*

Audience: *Heads, Subject Leaders, SLT, Governors, HLTAs.*
Cost: *£180 per delegate, with reduction of £100 per person for organizations sending two or more delegates.*
How to book: admin@howedell.herts.sch.uk
See School website for directions!

What gave Howe Dell the credibility to lead a conference?

Was it the new building? No. The curriculum development had been actively evolving for two years before our relocation and had involved staff awareness- raising even prior to that. This became evident in the conclusions of the first 2007 Hertfordshire University report, when the impact of ESD on the School community was evaluated in terms of attitudinal change:

> 'The establishment of the Howe Dell School learning community on sustainable development can act as an example to other schools regarding means of addressing the ESD curriculum and can act as a benchmark on what can be achieved in a school. Much of the change had already occurred and been embedded in practice before the School actually moved premises, so there is little reason why the findings of this exploration should not be transferable to other institutions.'
>
> University of Hertfordshire, 2007

The full report is available via the School website, where it is also documented that we had achieved our first Eco Schools Green Flag award, without the benefits of a purpose built-building. This clearly demonstrates the relevance of our curriculum development beyond our immediate community.

Certainly, a high-profile new build was a point of reference for

Hertfordshire, but at times was not always an advantage. Indeed, I recall a project manager once stating to visitors with strong design backgrounds: 'It's like Marmite: you either love it or hate it!'

So what successes could be utilized elsewhere?

◆ The day began with a key note speech from me, establishing the vision
◆ Our Facilities Manager gave an excellent overview of the principles behind our unique building and how the technologies work together to reduce our carbon footprint.
◆ There were tours by pupils, true ambassadors for the School.
◆ Useful presentations on assessment and Ofsted expectations gave a national perspective and were followed by a locally sourced lunch, through a Hertfordshire-based company called Foodsmiles, whose details can be found at www.foodsmiles.com.
◆ Asking our county catering team if they would like to do this was more costly than catering in-house, but celebrated our county provision and was one less hassle to worry about on the day, leaving our staff and pupils free to answer questions.
◆ Contacting Fair Trade, Wild Life Trust, county supplies and other local and national providers meant we had stalls for people to visit to resource projects or gain new information.
◆ RES have wonderful teaching resources on their website www.res-group.com. Telephone 0845 481 2856.

Give everybody a role to enhance the sense of shared ownership

The collating of delegates, fees and all other administration was left to Mel, who is now my Office Manager. This meant that there was consistency of approach and the overview was well organized from an administrative point of view by one person. It also raised the credibility of a non-teaching member of the leadership team. The workshops in the afternoon, set up in classrooms, with resources and children's work available, incccllluded the following.

◆ Integrating ESD within the curriculum.
◆ 0–5 and ESD via School and community.
◆ Training overseas and its impact on Geography provision.

◆ Early years and extended schools – ESD opportunities within and beyond the school day.
◆ ICT – trail blazing projects enriching ESD and our ICT provision map.
◆ Staff were sensitively paired, not only for expertise but to provide new partnership opportunities. Hence in some cases teachers from two different key stages worked together on a shared presentation. On other occasions, the teaching skills of a colleague supported the presentation skills of a non-teaching member of staff, who in return informed the Foundation Stage teacher in one particular paired presentation, of a greater awareness of community cohesion and family learning.

The day was very successful and was evaluated thoroughly by a researcher from NCSL who participated in the day itself and was interested in reviewing how I had demonstrated change leadership.

'Before the conference and during the early sessions, staff were anxious about their presentations. By the end of the day they had visibly grown in confidence. This was a good example of the ongoing delegation of responsibilities. A month later the staff were ready to do it again.'

NCSL Bob Curtis, 2009

What the report also acknowledges is that nothing stands still at Howe Dell, and on the day of the conference I accepted that the next phase was already needed: our current curriculum was out of date! That doesn't mean that the next day we were 'back to the drawing board'! Our creativity strand was launched by me booking tickets for all those involved in the day to see Michael Morpurgo's *War Horse* and then to gradually build in sustainable change through staff meeting, INSET and non-contact time for subject leaders. More importantly, whether Senior Leader or Newly Qualified Teacher, Secretary or Facilities Manager, we all enjoyed a shared treat as a result of the conference, but it was still with a focus on the next steps in learning.

In the words of a colleague of mine, Chris Wheatley, we all need to have a 'USP' – a unique selling point. At his school, Candleby Lane in Nottingham, it is bringing the community into the school to enrich an innovative enterprise curriculum. Through a visit to his organization, my team have seen this at first hand and reflected on our own practice at many levels.

Any good Head is proud of their school: it becomes your child, a living organism to be nurtured. At Howe Dell, this philosophy is owned by all, but shared too. This could mean that we become the stimulus for others to follow and to a certain extent, that's fine. When asked by a journalist from the *Times Educational Supplement* what was most important about her school, Tilly, aged 10, replied, 'We'll lead the way and others will follow. We don't realize we're saving the World because we're having so much fun.'

That impassioned view from a child encapsulates our success. From the proceeds of the conference's £4,500 approximate profit, the staff trip to the West End rewarded their commitment; and £2,500 is committed to creating a mobile model demonstrating the sustainable features of the site, planned by a link ESD governor and Facilities Manager.

And the children? They were presented with a Wii with a series of games to reinforce fitness and life skills, which is used weekly by the class with the best attendance.

Do we have everything in place? Almost – but we still take children and staff to other venues to learn from good practice elsewhere. Our next steps continue to include learning from good practice from others locally, nationally and overseas. Most recently, Year 6 used technology to contribute towards an international debate; a previous class, with the directive from a class teacher, have been able to join a G20 Debate on potential environmental issues of international significance. This is essential if we are to grow strong global citizens to have a say in preserving a sometimes fragile earth.

Further developments

◆ Use a local wildlife area and invite local schools to attend an eco conference. This was led by Howe Dell, but deliberately not hosted on site, using a shared resource for pond dipping, sketching, poetry, observation and a chance to reflect. This was filmed and presented to community leaders with input from each school as a means of pupil voice proposing a 'greener future' for their town.

◆ Visit the Eco Schools site. The bronze and silver awards are based on self-assessment and will give excellent audit tools for developing provision. The Eco Schools Green Flag we have achieved twice, the first at our early site: so it's not about state of the art buildings – it's about impact and ownership. Link with local secondary schools to provide work placements with a focus on your USP. We host daily and indeed block placements for students to enrich curriculum provision at Key Stage 3 and 4.

- Contact your local university to 'market' your USP – especially education or psychology departments. A piece of research from a reputable organization reaffirms the value of doing something differently.
- For school fetes and other events, add stalls with good eco credentials, whether that be produce form local farms, food cooked by families from diverse ethnic background or trendy accessories with an ESD twist.
- Additional materials available:
  - ✓ The curriculum – www.howedell.herts.sch.uk.
  - ✓ Curriculum and DVD of all training materials used for conference available via admin@howedell.herts.sch.uk (£25.00).
  - ✓ NCSL Report Leadership Change – see School website.
  - ✓ Two University of Hertfordshire research projects – see School website.

11 | Becoming an Outstanding School: Thinking Outside the Box, Not Ticking Boxes

Like many schools, fund raising takes different forms at Howe Dell. One opportunity arose from a child who wanted to do something positive, following a national disaster in Haiti.

Assemblies were shared in Key Stages, to make the content age appropriate, and as a result, families were asked to bring in what they could afford, to add to a world map.

This was left in a corridor, unsupervised for a week: pennies, £5 notes and every coin between the two were left with the aim of covering the world map with donations.

Why is this outstanding? Because it was left unsupervised, a developing display, a clear expectation of honesty and trust. It symbolized the acceptance that we were growing global citizens, who accepted rights, roles and responsibilities, as outlined in our eco enriched curriculum.

How to manage the balance of bureaucracy versus vision

I have never left the site after a busy day worrying over a form not completed, but do have concerns from time to time about the wellbeing of a child, when they are beyond the School gates. The focus of leadership must be the priority of making a positive difference to children's learning and life chances – otherwise what are we doing in schools?

What is clear is that if a form is very important and it has been completed incorrectly – or indeed forgotten – it is always somebody's job at local authority level to chase you for it!

Other items within an in-tray may easily be relegated to the category of 'If I have nothing else of importance to do with my day, I'll complete or read this'. Usually paperwork can be sorted into:

◆ Do it (because it matters to a child, staff or the school).
◆ Delegate it (because someone else knows more about this).
◆ Dump it (or recycle if you are a sustainable school!).

This is not new advice, but for the inexperienced leader it is easy to become overwhelmed by emails and paperwork and forget what a child looks like. Hence the value of the 'Sustainable School' having distributive leadership. At times, the Head's role becomes that of a facilitator, a critical friend and an adviser if needed. But be prepared to coach these newly empowered leaders to whom you have delegated, so that they too have permission to 'Do, Delegate or Dump', according to their own workloads.

Creative thinking for project management – a route map from good to outstanding

Whether fund raising or developing a curriculum, the difference between good and outstanding practice is to do with innovation and clarity. But be reassured, 'Genius is 99 per cent perspiration, 1 per cent inspiration' (Albert Einstein).

Successful creative planning encourages the leader to be:

◆ Specific about what is to be achieved via smart objectives.
◆ Receptive to ideas offered which enhance the initial concept and encourages wider ownership.
◆ Clear how the impact will be evaluated.
◆ Motivational with
    ✓ Colleagues
    ✓ Children.

Ideas come and go but the enduring phrase, always said at our School with a smile, if at times the occasional raised eyebrow, remains, 'only at Howe Dell'. Well, that's not the case. There are wonderful examples of creative planning ensuring good schools become outstanding, usually in organizations where bureaucratic blinkers are removed and a few choice risks are taken.

An example: not a shaggy dog story!

Through the Suggestion Box, a child asked if we could have a 'Pet Day'. To make this a successful vehicle for learning ...

◆ The aims to raise money for Guide Dogs for the Blind and provide motivational purposes for writing were published.
◆ It was thoroughly risk assessed.
◆ Prior notice was given to parents.
◆ Teachers managed individual visits to site of adults accompanying larger pets (from cats to pony and trap) and had the right to refuse if child or pet safety was a concern. This is far more practical than one person co-ordinating all visits.
◆ Everyone could dress up as an animal, donating to charity for the privilege.

Where it evolved to embrace a wider ownership was when the staff excitedly reported that all 78 would dress as dalmatians, if I would come as Cruella de Vil.

Making Learning Memorable: Learning through the day included parents arriving for class appointments with pets, whilst all children visited our zoo for the day in our hall! Numeracy opportunities included children counting the money raised, being challenged to audit the range and number of pets brought in, from horse to tortoise, and to count the staff and pupils dressed as dalmations, estimating the number of spots, to report back to Cruella!

◆ Was the day motivational and memorable to all involved?
◆ Did it give real purposes for writing?
◆ Did it raise awareness of animal care (through visits from animal agency walkers and independent research)?
◆ Did it raise money for charity?

All of these questions are firmly answered with a 'Yes', but, more importantly, the laughter and sense of shared fun with learning demonstrate tangibly what outstanding provision is all about.

From good to outstanding

Not every day can be a 'Pet Day', however, there needs to be a boldness of approach which encourages stakeholders to believe that the leader knows what creative provision looks like and will recognize outstanding practice, when it is achieved.

The role of development planning is key here: by focusing on an aim and breaking it into tasks, it can be ticked off in 'bite size' chunks. This is demonstrated in the development plan extract overleaf.

The planning process needs to have particular strands in order to demonstrate that 'no stone is left unturned' by reviewing aims for:

◆ Leadership.
◆ Every Child Matters.
◆ Curriculum.
◆ Self-evaluation.
◆ Financial forecasting (five years).
◆ Vision, aims.

Progress or attainment?

When considering the levels of attainment in a school, it is crucial that there is clarity from teachers as to what levels are evident within the cohort. This sounds obvious, but the distribution of attainment is key when considering:

◆ How might I utilize a teaching assistant more effectively?
◆ Which group will the teacher focus upon?
◆ What are the next steps in learning?

Aim 1 To continue to develop staff and knowledge and expertise in 'Creativity'.

	Activity	Lead responsibility	Timeline	Resource implications	Success criteria
Task 1 Awareness raising	Year group Creative Days across School when off timetable to extend a theme or concept. This needs to be skills based to ensure transferrable to other learning experiences	ED and KS Leaders.	One day every half term.	Staff meeting time in KS meetings to share ideas.	More confidence to try 'new skills' – more creative use of curriculum. Report to Curriculum Committee and learning walk involving governors and pupils. Portfolios and self-evaluation review impact on attitude of staff, parents and pupils.

Therefore, as well as demonstrating differentiation in the medium- and short-term planning, it is important to log the levels of attainment to accompany lesson observations, so that the observer (whether a school leader, an adviser or inspector) can accurately determine that this teacher:

◆ sets high yet attainable targets.
◆ knows 'next steps' in learning.

This is especially important if there is a large group of pupils who may be achieving below national average scores.

Tracking of progress becomes ever more important. For example, a specialist education provider may have outstanding teaching and excellent progress, but attainment well below national expectations. Hence, this is not about ticking boxes for the sake of bureaucracy, but rather about enabling a good school to flourish as outstanding with child-focused data to support that process.

What progress to track and when

To demonstrate that the leader has a clear vision in developing a school from good to outstanding, a profile of teaching quality is essential in demonstrating prior knowledge of strong teachers – and where support is needed. Furthermore, via lesson observations and performance management documentation, it is clear what steps have been offered to support such staff.

At Howe Dell, we assess children's learning in a manner which is age/stage relevant each half term, initially annotating outcomes in Writing, Science and Maths assessments for the attention of the Head. Now, due to the empowerment of strong subject leaders, it is *they* who review this information. Their findings across the School determine:

◆ Cohort/whole School needs.
◆ Focus for future training/staff meetings.
◆ Resourcing priorities.

At the end of each term, the second assessment is input into a computer programme so that:

◆ Reading comprehension is also assessed.

♦ The attainment profile across a cohort can be seen.
♦ The progress against targets set can be established.
♦ Key successes can be case studied.
♦ Pupils who are static are picked up quickly and intervention is reviewed in the light of this.

As a result, our termly progress review is shared. Initially this was the work of the Head, but due to successful coaching, subject leaders and inclusion co-ordinators play a vital role. The process is as follows·

♦ Number of children static, those making 1/3, 2/3 level progress or indeed more is clearly logged.
♦ Consideration that if 2/3 level is considered good progress, then percentages as well as number of children standardize the resulting report.

Worked example showing extract of report for Reading from progress review

Note: Child's name replaced with initials for governors' version and date of report removed, all to ensure confidentiality.

Class & number of tracked pupils	No Progress to Date	1/3	2/3	3/3	4/3	5/3	Comments regarding key children given in detail to class teachers and summarised for staff discussion and planning and to inform core subject leaders	APS
Y2 54 pupils %	1 1.85	4 7.41	20 31.04	13 24.07	10 18.51	6 11.11	Includes Child A: child with SEN statement, only static pupil in cohort. Traveller pupils show excellent progress. Child B attendance ongoing concern – EWO aware. Children C–F – 4/3 level progress.	5.67 ↑↑
Y5 28 pupils %	1 3.57	4 14.29	6 21.43	13 46.43	2 7.14	2 7.14	Child G – 2/3 level progress – SEN Child H – 3/3 level progress – SEN Lots of examples of excellent teaching impacting on individual pupils.	5.21 ↑↑
Y6 (SATS) 29 pupils %	1 3	5 17	11 38	7 24	3 11	2 7	Children I,J – 5/3 level progress. Children K, L, M – 4/3 level progress. Child N – static SEN. Joined mid -KS2.	4.83 ↑↑

Y6 attainment: teacher assessment

L4+ 26/29 = 89.66 per cent
L4a 24/29 = 82.79 per cent
L5+ 20/29 = 68.97 per cent

Y6 SATs tests

L4+ = 94 per cent
L5+ = 77 per cent
Exceptional progress and attainment with 97 per cent showing two levels progress and 63 per cent showing more than that, from Y2. 16.7 per cent make 3 levels progress OR MORE!

Level 5 exceptionally high
Y5 attainment

L4b+ 18/28 = 64.29 per cent
L4a+ 15/28 = 53.57 per cent
L5+ 9/28 = 32.14 per cent
L4b+ pupils being well placed for exceeding targets set previous autumn, based on attainment and KS1 performance of this cohort.

Note

Clearly a strength of the School. All year groups almost meeting or dramatically exceeding good progress APS of 4.0. The continued author visits through Wonder Days have inspired children to read and provided extended opportunities for families to enjoy stories as a shared and social activity in Y5 and the investment of Barrington Stokes, Specific Learning Difficulty (SpLD) resources and quality shared readers have had impact.

◆ *In Key Stage 2 Reading Workshops including Newspapers have extended able readers.*
◆ *Developed use of ICT has encouraged children to read for research purposes (see Y6 ICT award winning project).*
◆ *Independent research is a biproduct of out ESD curriculum in and beyond school.*
◆ *Nevertheless, School has committed to 'Every Child a Reader' project for less able Y1 children who in Reception class already were displaying need, including Traveller children.*

An example of a pro forma for progress review is available on the companion website.

What do I need to demonstrate rigorous tracking rather than a bureaucratic exercise?

Consider where your priorities are by reviewing:

◆ Online data over three years.
◆ Look at lesson plan outcomes. Are there emerging themes for development?
◆ Consider 'vulnerable' groups which demonstrate 'best practice provision'. This will show areas of historical need for your organization, but also where interventions are in place.
◆ Consider reviewing Year 4 data at year end as a 'health test' for progress from Key Stage 1 to 2.

Most importantly, by using the pro forma and modelling data reporting for consistency enables shared learning from subject leaders and smart use of the Head's time. In so doing, the story of your organization is clearly logged, but specific to its needs.

And remember, the greatest investment is always your team. With staff believing that we can make a difference to children's learning every day, the love of learning and broadening of possibilities continues to extend. More importantly, encouraging staff to think of new ways of revisiting basic skills through community or curricular projects, with a strong emphasis on raising attainment in personal skills, ensures that the impact against a shared focus can be measured, whatever the vehicle might be to facilitate this.

Nevertheless, there is also a need to recognize that no one can be driven on full throttle endlessly. The chance for 'smiley days', cancelled meetings, additional 'golden time', treats as part of training, high tea and cake, all reinforce for the adults the glory of doing the exceptional and being celebrated for it.

Key points for consideration

◆ What would the lasting impression of your school be to a visitor? Ask a colleague from another school to do a learning walk for you to:
    ✓ Practise selling what a colleague of mine calls the school's unique selling point. See Candleby Lane, Nottingham, for how they have shaped a community: www.ccls.notts.sch.uk.
    ✓ See things through fresh eyes, perhaps noticing a display that

has been up too long, or that teaching assistants' questioning is truly exceptional.

◆ Recognize bureaucracy and box ticking can be valuable in moving an organization forward, but if important enough and forgotten, it is likely you will be reminded!

◆ Establish systems and processes to review attainment, progress and the quality of teaching and learning, as this is our 'bread and butter'. Leadership can hardly be satisfactory, let alone outstanding, if this is not in place.

◆ Have examples, supported with self-evaluative evidence of excellent practice. A Pet Day may not be planned for when Ofsted arrive – but be sure to be able to demonstrate its *impact*.

◆ Be clear with shared responsibility for data analysis, coached by the Head, that the focus on raising standards is shared and understood.

◆ Consider how tracking is fed back to a range of audiences. For example, curriculum governors may value the progress review but it needs to be without trace to a particular child, to avoid conflict with data protection.

◆ Sustainability is key: mapping out when assessments, big events, skill practice are happening is crucial to avoid staff sick with exhaustion.

◆ Give yourself and your team a chance to enjoy the journey and celebrate the wellbeing of the team that make this possible. Sometimes this is about demonstrating with the leader's own life–work balance: you are not the person there first in the morning *and* leaving last at night. Otherwise, what kind of role model are you for the 'Sustainable School'?

◆ Lastly, in thinking outside the box, keep the learning focus shared by encouraging creative thinking from others, but with outcomes embedded into the vision for progress and development that you have all signed up to. That way, smarter working processes and distributive leadership with maximum impact is assured.

12 | Sharing the Vision, Extending the Impact: Best Practice for All

It's a leadership training day. In the past, when budget allowed, these have been off site at a venue which is looked forward to, as much as the content and the chance to work together.

Chris, my lead teacher for Key Stage 1, is sharing outcomes from the task set before the day 'to share with the team evidence of how a colleague has developed their leadership capacity'.

She is a wonderful teacher, passionate speaker and holds our attention as she explains why Gail, a relatively new teaching assistant, came to mind.

Gail is still new to the School environment, being a qualified chef who previously ran her own business. In the last year, she has developed wonderful relationships with the children, especially those who are most vulnerable. She has gone from working with small groups, to confidently leading a class, preparing resources and completing individual education plans for special needs pupils. Gail played 'The Last Post' on a cornet for our Remembrance Service, she runs the Let's Get Cooking club for upper Key Stage 2 ...

As Chris talked, quite emotionally at times, colleagues listened attentively, before adding other characteristics about Gail: she is committed to charity work with the homeless, she helps in the office, comes in at short notice to help resolve a staffing crisis in the snow, to ensure the holiday club could still run.

Gail is truly an example of what makes leadership distributive and owned at Howe Dell. But so too is Chris: her patience in modelling teaching, pastoral and behaviour management is clearly reflected in someone she now line manages.

Yes, sharing the vision and enabling people to utilize skills and personalities encourages stronger impact and reaffirms what best practice looks like.

Other members of the leadership team shared equally inspirational stories. The task outline is available on the web site.

So what is the lasting impact?

◆ Capturing these 'good news' stories can be uplifting, but to have lasting impact they need sharing with a wider audience. This can be through the School website, a PowerPoint, School newsletter – or assembly. Consider any sensitive issues before deciding how and where to publicize.

◆ A certificate created by a member of the Children's Council can be presented with the member of staff being named and a brief reason as to why they are an inspirational leader.

◆ If budget allows, flowers or a bottle of wine to say thank you at an INSET day – or a 'Smiley Day' of extra leave can reaffirm to colleagues how this impacts on our provision.

◆ On a less public level, the member of the leadership team can explain to the nominated colleague which aspects of what they do was key in putting their name forward. Jayne, a teaching assistant with many years' experience but new to Foundation Stage, was nominated. Despite an injury outside work making her cautious in working with some very challenging 4 year old boys, she has had huge impact on their behaviour, attainment and the sanity of the class teacher! She was so thrilled with the feedback, she asked for a copy to put in her Professional Development Portfolio – a new idea introduced the year before by our Deputy. This not only reaffirmed the value of positive recognition, but also the credence given to the Deputy's recently introduced initiative for performance management.

◆ Finally, ensuring that the Head speaks to each of those nominated, and leadership team members doing the same, reinforces the power of the message: 'You matter and so does what you do in our organization.'

Why is this approach essential?

It is a well-known fact that it takes fewer muscles to smile than to frown: this enables smiles to be shared and puts into context minor differences of opinion or petty issues, in order to focus on the 'bigger picture'. Linking vision building to a staff training day reinforces the ownership by all.

From a Head's perspective, you have 'ready made disciples to spread the word'. These people are ambassadors who would make excellent mentors for new staff, as part of the induction process. It also makes the whole vision building and school development more sustainable, as there is a reliance on the team approach, rather than on one person and one person alone.

This is key when considering succession leadership. Ideally this should be discussed before anyone on the leadership team has begun to apply for jobs elsewhere, but gives opportunity for healthy dialogue and openness, to avoid insecurity or 'in-house politics' getting in the way of school improvement. No one, including the Head, should be more important than the organization they serve. (It is humbling at times to remember that we are but custodians for a while, in the life of a school.)

How can leadership opportunities be evidenced within your School or setting?

Another task used on the leadership day (the agenda for which is available via the companion website) involved staff bringing an artefact which reinforced what colleagues felt represented excellence at Howe Dell.

Examples included the following.

- ◆ Badges worn by Children's Council and Eco Squad to reinforce the exciting opportunities for pupil voice.
- ◆ A letter from a mum who was caught out by cancelled trains, but thanked Day Care staff who stayed late to care for her twins and were kind and reassuring when she eventually arrived.
- ◆ A photo of a role play area in Year 2, which was totally child initiated, has been a resource for toddlers to 7-year-olds. It successfully included the less able, but extended Sean.

Amidst bugs and leaves in the jungle-inspired area, Sean wrote in his Jungle Shop:
'Please do not take things *without paying, otherwise you will have a free ride in a police car.'*

Meanwhile, my offered resource for the task, often used at Howe Dell, was *Elmer the Patchwork Elephant*. The patchwork colours represent the many skills and talents, but also the gaps in knowledge and understanding, we all feel at some time. In a successful sustainable school, built on many people's talents, no one is expected to be the expert in all things; moreover, the harder aspects of the job become manageable by those who have those skills already, in a culture where teamwork is cascaded.

Is there any data to support impact?

Qualitative case studies are a rich evidence resource to inform school improvement but also to celebrate successes within and beyond the curriculum. When looking specifically at measuring staff wellbeing or quantitative evidence of successfully sharing the vision in a healthy working environment, the following routes may be of use.

◆ Consider sick records – are there any groups which have a better health record than others? Key staff with ongoing ill health is a separate issue, but happy, motivated colleagues are rarely off sick.

◆ Log, year on year, the number of staff who attend out-of-hours events, not individually but collectively. This year, when setting up the 'Howe Dell's Got Talent' event, I was delighted that Amanda (yet another star celebrated by the Leadership Team) not only attended the event but gave up lunchtime to support the Children's Council, judging the auditions. A clear example of how School and Day Care teams have gained an improved shared understanding.

◆ As well as maintaining a Visitor's Log, already mentioned, to show how your organization trains and inspires others beyond the school community, also collate the times when staff have been to other schools or worked for the local authority, in order to cascade good practice. This is excellent professional development for the individual and can be a good source of revenue. In years when 'claw back' of surplus funds was threatened by the local authority, I agreed with governors that any such income was additional to the school budget share and should therefore be kept separate from the general account. This is formally ring fenced and reported on to governors annually so that the audit trail is clear, but gives more flexibility in spending of funds. Most recently, my consultancy fees have paid for internationally acclaimed author and illustrator Jackie Morris to revisit the School and for large scale prints of her work to be bought and

framed. This inspirational visitor in her 'Dragon Van' arriving from Wales on World Book Day for a Wonder Day therefore has lasting impact beyond her visit.

Grow a team, knowing you will set it free

'I trust you to make that decision' is very powerful as an approach, but takes time, patience and an acceptance that sometimes people outgrow their role, even if that continues to adapt. Like seed dispersal, the loss of strong members of staff who move on to lead their own organizations is natural and healthy. It doesn't mean it is not at times inconvenient, it does not mean that the person is not missed, but it spreads the magic to new organizations and so the cycle begins again.

Sometimes, like Nina in Chapter 2, people leave but return at a later date with new skills and credibility. Sometimes an ex-colleague from the past seeks you out and joins your organization in a new capacity, which neither of you could have predicted in your previous working relationship. This was the case when Emma, a colleague team taught with me when I was a new Deputy ten years previously, was successfully appointed to lead Foundation Stage at Howe Dell. Much has changed, but her loyalty, her belief in the shared vision and her determination to see the best in everyone (child or adult) has been a constant from which we can all learn.

Whilst encouraging schools to be hosts to the NPQH National College of School Leadership trainee headship programme, it would be hypocritical to not then encourage our own Deputy to embark on the programme. Her strategic perspective has developed and she has just begun her own headship. This is a testament to growing leaders – evidence of its success.

Occasionally, strong leaders have the unenviable task of giving strong candidates after interview the news that they were not appointed. By giving open and honest feedback and offering to remain in touch, three of the four shortlisted Deputy applicants at a previous school were successfully appointed within the term. One came back to talk through her presentation prior to another interview. It is vital as leaders that this feedback is honest and supportive. Often candidates feel crushed and defeated: managing this well has meant that some have been recommended to other schools or even successfully reapplied at Howe Dell for future positions.

Be reasonable to yourself – there will be times when growth and change is difficult

This can be the part of leadership which creates most challenge: people have babies at times not always convenient to school development planning! Yet, enabling this to be a *supportive process* can give a leader the chance to think differently and to support staff wellbeing creatively by:

◆ Using a local Children's Centre to sign post local child care facilities.
◆ Is it possible to subsidize costs for staff, thus making it more probable they will return after maternity leave? Yes, it's a cost, but the payback is huge. We now have Day Care on site and this in principal means a young mum could still be breastfeeding her baby but return to work.
◆ Could two returning parents share a child minder, local to school?
◆ Is there capacity in a job share for the occasional absence due to the sickness of a child to be covered by the job share partner and then time 'paid back'? This avoids costs to school and aids consistency for the children in your setting.
◆ How is paternity leave organized? Yes, it can be in a block, but if it is negotiated with the Year 6 teacher who is an expectant father that he takes this time in shorter periods, consistency can remain for those children in preparation for exams and secondary school and it may also be useful to the newly formed family too.

The impact? Very few days lost through staff sickness or absence due to their children. *However,* I have to say that when our secretary returned for two days a week, having had twins, to announce four months later that she was pregnant again, it *did* set the challenge to a new level!

When might things start to go wrong?

Sometimes the distributive leadership approach might empower to the point where there are breakdowns in communication or 'silo working' to the detriment of the overall organisation. These have been minimized by weekly half-hour leadership team meetings and group emails to inform and update colleagues. Realistically, they do happen, but are usually unpicked quickly. Interestingly, when considering growth resulting in staff restructuring, the team were asked what they valued most. Their replies were as follows.

♦ A regular and clear communication.
♦ A team approach, sharing knowledge, skills and support.
♦ Openness and approachability from the senior leadership team.
♦ Knowledge of the families at every level of responsibility.

So, it really isn't rocket science, I don't feel I am best placed to theorize on what this means. It simply makes sense and encourages growth within our schools at all levels.

Last thoughts

My leadership style remains multifaceted, but William Q. Judges' analysis of the executive leader has made this clearer to define. What follows, will be shaped by the leadership *within*. I will always aim to have the passion and enthusiasm to represent Howe Dell, but the last two years have given me the opportunity to grow leaders. These amazing people can take responsibility for *sharing* the management on a day-to-day basis, but also to contribute to *shaping the vision of our future*. They have evolved from managers to leaders in their own right, and staff and children beyond the leadership focus group are now impacting on shared vision and ethos. It is also right and healthy for staff to move on to lead elsewhere and maybe take some of the obvious successful strategies with them, but also in time, come to realise how the more subtle infrastructure to our ethos has given it depth and credibility. By losing strong staff, others step up to seize the mantle, new staff too come into an organisation and enjoy what perhaps can too easily be taken for granted if not seen through fresh eyes. All of this might create challenges but revisits and reviews the Sustainable School model. In the Preface I referred to Collins' analogy of a leadership journey and bus travel: in conclusion, perhaps air travel is closer to my learning experience here.

On a site from whence the first Comet passenger aeroplane flew, my leadership required a steep acceleration to begin with, but I am not alone. I recognize that leaders at Howe Dell Children's Centre and School are ensuring clear direction towards our departure from Howe Dell, The Runway, towards the future that awaits us! Some will move on, leaving a stronger, more resilient setting as a result of their involvement. They will move not because of years of service, or frustration caused by lack of opportunity, but because they are ready to lead under their own banner. This is testament to the distributive leadership model in any 'Sustainable School'. In the words of Sir Winston Churchill:

'Now this is not the end. It is not even the beginning of the end. But it is, perhaps, the end of the beginning.'

Speech November 1942

Bibliography

Allman, Paulo, 'The Nature and Development of Adult Learning' in M. Tight (ed.), *Adult Learning and Education,* Croom Helm, 1983.

Anderson, Alan H., Barker, Dennis and Critten, Peter, *Effective Self Development,* Blackwell, 1996.

Beare, H, *Creating the Future School: Student Outcomes and the Reform of Education,* Routledge Falmer, 2001.

Bergmann, Sherrel and Allenbrough, Judith, *Lead Me, I Dare You!: Managing Resistance to School Change,* Eye on Education Inc., 2007.

Bloomfield, Peter, Hoad, Bridget, Allen, Rosemary and Rees, Mary, *Developing Awareness of Education for Sustainable Development: Foundations for our Future. A Report on the Sustainable Development Learning Journey of the Howe Dell School Community, 2006 to 2007,* University of Hertfordshire, 2007.

Collins, J. G., *Good to Great: Why Some Companies Make the Leap – and Others Don't,* Harper Business, 2001.

Fink, Dean, *Leadership for Mortals,* SAGE, 2005.

Hall, Valerie, *Dancing on the Ceiling: A Study of Women Managers in Education,* Paul Chapman, 1996.

Hargreaves, Andy and Fink, Dean, *Sustainable Leadership,* John Wiley and Sons, 2006.

Heerkens, Gary H., *Project Management,* McGraw – Hill, 2002.

Hissey, J., *Old Bear,* Red Fox, 1998.

Kipling, R., *IF* (Brother Square Toes) Poem, 1898.

Machiavelli, N. *The Prince,* Mentor Press (original publication 1513), 1962.

McKee, David, *Elmer the Patchwork Elephant,* Anderson Press, 1991.

Parker Follet, Mary, *Creative Experience,* Longman Green, 1924.

Simon-Rosenthal, Cindy, *When Women Lead,* OUP (New York), 1998.

Weston, Kathryn, Thornton, Mary and Bloomfield, Peter, *Howe Dell School and Children's Centre: Exploring Their Impact on the Wider*

Community in Terms of Sustainable Development., University of Hertfordshire. May 2009.

Whalley, M., *Characteristics of Integrated Centre Leaders,* NPQICL Training Materials 2007, 1999.

Whalley, M., and Whitaker, P., *Whalley – Whitaker leadership Construct,* NPQICL Training Materials 2000, 2007.

Index